To Rob, my own great ... ope,

An incitement to ... ?

ever there we ... ! £2.49
-28

Merry Christmas '94

kisses

Richard

xxx

D0282865

WAKE UP
BRITAIN!

WAKE UP
BRITAIN!

A LATTER-DAY PAMPHLET

Paul Johnson

WEIDENFELD AND NICOLSON

London

First published in Great Britain in 1994
by Weidenfeld & Nicolson

The Orion Publishing Group Ltd
Orion House
5 Upper Saint Martin's Lane
London WC2H 9EA

ISBN 0 297 81484 2

A catalogue record for this book is available
from the British Library

Typeset by Deltatype Ltd, Ellesmere Port, S. Wirral
Printed and bound in Great Britain by
Butler & Tanner Ltd, Frome and London

Contents

CHAPTER ONE

A Good Country with One Thing Missing –
Democracy

*W*hy is Britain an unhappy country today? The answer can be given in five words: because it is insufficiently democratic. More democracy will not solve all our problems. But it will eradicate some of them and mitigate many others. That is the thesis of this tract for the times.

The English were the first nation in the world to develop durable representative institutions. The emergence of parliament, from its foreshadowing in Anglo-Saxon times, through its Norman and Angevin prototypes, to its regular functioning in the fourteenth century, is the historical achievement of which we can be most proud. But Britain took a long time to become a democracy even in theory. Oddly enough, my early life spanned the period when the last reforms were put in place. In 1928, the year I was born, women between twenty-one and thirty, the so-called 'flappers', got the vote for the first time, which at last gave women absolute equality with men in both parliamentary and local government elections. But it was not until 1948, when I was nineteen, that the law abolished plural voting, under which owners of businesses could vote in more than one parliamentary constituency and, in local elections, sometimes cast as many as 13 lawful votes. My old friend Aneurin Bevan always held that British democracy did not mature until 1945, when the Labour Party, which he equated with the popular will, first achieved an absolute majority in the House of Commons. I maintain, on the contrary, that Britain has yet to become a fully-fledged functioning democracy, and therein lies our trouble.

The tribulations of Britain in the 1990s sometimes seem almost unbearable to one of my generation and upbringing. My parents were middle-class Roman Catholics. Both were teachers by profession (as, later, were my two elder sisters, one at a grammar school, one at an Oxford college). At the time of his death, when I was thirteen, my father was headmaster of the art school at Burslem in the Potteries. He was also a gifted painter, mainly in watercolours, an etcher and engraver. He believed, perhaps optimistically, that art not only enriched the world but elevated and improved human nature. If men and women were surrounded by beautiful, well-made objects, even in their daily life, their moral conduct would improve. This assumption, which derived from the Arts and Crafts Movement of the previous century, was his secular credo, and he applied it enthusiastically to his work. Many of the boys and girls taught at his school went on to occupy senior positions, both as craftsmen-designers and as managers in the local pottery industry, which was then enormous and sold its wares all over the world. My father felt he was privileged to hold a key position in the business of using applied art to improve humanity. He never hesitated to impress, both on his staff and still more on his pupils, the weight of their responsibilities. Like countless other middle-class people in those days, he saw life in terms of duties. One's work was not just a job, but a calling: God, in his infinite wisdom, set us specific tasks, and woe betide us if we did not devote all our energies and abilities to discharging them. His own calling he saw as a high one, which gave him infinite delight as well as the moral satisfaction of doing God's will. Though his salary was modest, his family large and his means small, he considered himself a most fortunate man.

I was thus brought up in an atmosphere of joyous idealism, not uncommon in those times. In my family by far the most important thing was religion; after that came art and education. Nothing else really mattered, and all our resources and energies went into these two causes. We had little pocket money, few treats, indeed few material things of any kind, apart from books and pictures. My father was much involved in the design, building and decoration of an enormous church, which our ambitious and energetic parish priest was building near to our house. We were in and out of it many times during the week. The annual cycle of the liturgy governed our lives, punctuated by the great festivals of the church. A tenth of my father's income was devoted to religious purposes and much of the rest went on our education, which was of course at Catholic schools; those were absolute priorities.

Our religion was intimately connected with our patriotism. All the British were patriots in those days but the Catholics, for historical reasons, especially so. Our ancestors in the sixteenth century, and even after, had been accused of treason – and often tortured to death for it – because they acknowledged the spiritual supremacy of the Roman pontiff. They hotly disputed the charge at the time, and then and ever since Catholics have been anxious to demonstrate their loyalty to Crown and country by conspicuous service, in war and peace.

When the penal laws against Catholics were relaxed, the armed services were among the first professions to be thrown open to Papists, and they flocked to join them, especially the army. Catholics were also the first to volunteer in wartime. The day the First World War was declared, 4 August 1914, my mother's three brothers, and my father and his two brothers, all went together to the recruiting office to enlist. They regarded doing anything else as unthinkable. Again, on 3 September 1939, immediately after hearing Mr Chamberlain's speech declaring war on Germany, my elder brother went to enlist. He returned to announce he had got into a Hussar regiment and would be 'in the heavy tanks': I still recall the look of mingled pride and fear which flashed across my mother's face when he gave her this joyful news. My school, Stonyhurst, to which my parents contrived with great sacrifice to send me, was the oldest Catholic school in England, founded in 1592. The first two centuries of its existence had been spent in Flanders, for under the penal laws it was illegal for the Catholic gentry to educate their sons in their religion. But even in those times many Stonyhurst alumni served with distinction in the army. When the school at last was able to establish itself in England, the

Jesuit fathers encouraged the boys to devote their adult lives to the service of the country, notably in the armed forces, and from its inception the Officer Training Corps figured prominently in Stonyhurst life. In my day it was, next to the Church itself, the most important institution in the college, taken with the utmost seriousness. The school was particularly proud of its old boys' record for gallantry. The main boys' dining hall was hung with full-length portraits of former Stonyhurst pupils who had won the Victoria Cross. Shortly after I arrived at the school, we were woken up in the middle of the night – as it seemed to our dormitory – to be given the glorious news that yet another old boy had won the VC.

Neither my parents nor the Jesuits ever taught the evil doctrine 'My country right or wrong'. Quite the contrary. The patriotism I imbibed from earliest childhood was religious, indeed missionary. In ancient times, indeed until the end of the seventeenth century, many English believed that their nation had a special relationship with God: the English were a chosen people, an 'elect nation', entrusted by the Almighty with important tasks in the world, especially the work of enlightening the heathen and civilising the savages. This belief we transmitted to the Americans through the Pilgrim Fathers, who settled in Massachusetts to build 'a City on a Hill', to send out beacons of light into a dark hemisphere. But we in Britain also retained God's favour ourselves, and the important duties of reform and evangelism that went with it. As John Milton put it, when 'God is decreeing some new and great period in his Church . . . what does He do then but reveal Himself to his servants, and as his manner is, first to his Englishmen'.

At the time I was a boy and learning about our country, this belief had been demythologised and secularised, but it was still potent. In the early 1930s, the British Empire and Commonwealth was at its largest; it included many territories, such as Iraq and Palestine, which had been given to Britain and its dominions to administer under mandate from the League of Nations. It covered over a quarter of the earth's surface and its magnitude was brought home in countless maps, with the imperial possessions coloured in red, which hung in every nursery and schoolroom in the kingdom.

We were taught, and fervently believed, that the empire was the greatest in the history of the world, but not primarily because of its extent and military might. These we took for granted and rejoiced in. But we were still more proud of the moral qualities and purpose of the empire. My big sisters who (with my mother) showed me how to read and write, and taught me French and Latin, a little Greek and a great deal of history, always emphasised that our great empire, acquired with such enterprise and gallantry, was run entirely in the interests of its inhabitants of all races. It was an enlightened and liberal empire, creative and noble in its objects, its aim being to bring peace, justice, education, modern agriculture, transport, industry and, eventually, parliamentary government to all the peoples who composed it. It was thus an unprecedented artifact of Christian civilisation, and that was why God looked upon it with favour and assisted his Englishmen in their work of benevolent administration. This image of empire, implanted by my sisters, was reinforced in the classroom, whose walls were decorated by many imperial charts showing, sometimes with actual specimens behind cellophane screens, how the dominions and colonies grew coffee and tea, cotton and flax, bred sheep for wool and cattle for meat, and how these products, and the goods manufactured from them, passed through a benevolent worldwide network of trade, carried chiefly in British steamers, for the wealth, health and happiness of all.

It was a source of burning pride for little boys like myself in the 1930s that the British Empire, and especially the long arm of the Royal Navy, stretching to every river outlet and sea-coast in the world, had played the leading part in suppressing the atrocious slave trade and had eventually succeeded in abolishing slavery almost everywhere; that it kept the seas and oceans free of pirates and marauders of all kinds so that every nation on earth could trade in safety; and that it was, even now, carrying on the work of draining swamps and reducing malaria, building hospitals and clinics so that the world's poor could be vaccinated against smallpox, setting up dams and irrigation schemes to end famine, and coming to the rescue of people all over our planet who were the victims of plague, earthquakes, floods and volcanoes. Our empire was great, but it was also an empire of learning, science, engineering and mercy – and all these aspects were illustrated in our schoolroom charts.

I do not think I absorbed any political dogma as a child, other than those inherent in Catholicism. My father was conservative and voted Tory; my mother was more of a Gladstonian Liberal. Both regarded politics as a necessary evil whose positive function was to promote the well-being of 'the poor'. Just as they foresaw a distant day when all the peoples of the empire, by a mysterious symbiosis, would become like the British and begin to govern themselves, so they assumed that, gradually, 'the poor' would rise to middle-class standards of living and, more important, of culture. Academics call this the embourgeoisment of the proletariat, and it has now largely occurred, in material terms. It has also been accompanied, to a great extent, by a middle-class adoption of many working-class cultural and moral customs, a perverse process which would have horrified my father and indeed did horrify my mother, who survived to see it.

Where we lived, it was impossible not to be conscious of the existence of 'the poor' and indeed of a poverty which was the normal condition of existence. Materially, my family lived with marked frugality – there were no luxuries whatsoever – but we were conscious of being extremely fortunate compared to most others. North Staffordshire had been one of the earliest parts of Britain to industrialise itself. Its lunar landscape of thousands of small, bottle-shaped pot-banks had a late-eighteenth-century appearance and was already well on its way to becoming an industrial museum. At night the sky was fiery red and lit by flashes, as in a Loutherberg painting. By day the grim desolation of the industrial scene, with its workshops both ruined and active, its waste-tips and spoil-mountains, its black, stagnant pools, immense columns of smoke and steam, and its prevailing colours of iron grey and rich, corrupt brown, has left ineffaceable impressions on my visual memory. My father liked to paint it, as did his friend and confidant L. S. Lowry, though both preferred the cotton-mill townscape of Manchester, which they said was 'cleaner'.

The predominant characteristic of the potteries in those days was indeed filth. The air was full of smuts. My mother complained that our freshly-laundered white blouses and shirts were dirty as soon as we put them on. Keeping our hands and knees clean was a constant struggle. The workers and their children were grimy at all times, their clothes dingy and often ragged, except on Sundays. They smelt, not always but usually. The coal pits paid good wages and jobs on the many private industrial railways were also prized, but the potters, half of whom were young women, were one of the lowest-paid groups of workers in the country. In appearance and speech – the local vernacular was almost impenetrable – they seemed a different race. But there was never the smallest hint of class feeling that I was aware of. My parents were awed by the patience and good-nature of 'the poor'. What struck me was their cheerfulness and generosity. My bright red, curly hair often attracted attention when I was out for a walk and working men would hand me a penny. My mother always insisted I gave it back politely, which I was most reluctant to do.

So far as I could see, all 'the poor' went to Sunday services, most to nonconformist chapels, especially Primitive Methodist, but in growing numbers to our huge Catholic church, big enough to be a cathedral (as it now is). I was well aware of drunken shouts and reelings, even quarrels, on Saturday nights. But if there was any crime, it never impinged on our lives. I do not recall my parents ever locking the door, except when we went away on holiday. None of us ever had anything stolen or felt the slightest tinge of apprehension walking the streets, night or day. I can remember one solitary case of vandalism. A newly-planted tree in the street near our house had some of its bark stripped off, presumably by wicked boys. This outrage caused a sensation and the local plain-clothes detective conducted an investigation. It is the only time I have ever seen a sleuth use a magnifying glass. Nothing came of his efforts, but my sisters bound up the tree, which recovered, and the crime was never repeated.

This pre-war world of my childhood, with its privations but also with its stability, its security and its confident belief in the Christian moral framework of the world, upheld in great part by Britain and its empire, was shattered by that broadcast on 3

September 1939. We did not realise this at the time, or at least I did not. On the contrary: I secretly rejoiced. I was already, as I had been ever since I first learned to read, on a version of Froissart's *Chronicles*, a passionate student of history. It seemed to me that the historical process had somehow stopped a few years before I was born, and that nothing happening since qualified as real history. Now the mysterious Mr Chamberlain had started the historical clock ticking again and we were moving towards great events. So, may God forgive me, I welcomed the declaration of war.

But my father's face, as I noticed at the time, was grey with anxiety. He had been right through the First World War, had been wounded three times and fearfully gassed with phosgene. His lungs were permanently damaged. Within three years overwork, loss of staff, no petrol and the other consequences of wartime had killed him. My brother, so swift to enlist, emerged after six years disillusioned and damaged, his hearing gone; he, too, was not to live long. First the family's home went, then its members scattered and this diaspora, as it seems to me now, mirrored on a small scale the disintegration of the world of red on the map which Britain had seemed to rule.

Other changes followed, in relentless succession, to transform the world we had known. The post-war Labour government, and its successors, completed the fabrication of the welfare state which Lloyd George and Churchill had begun in the years before 1914. In doing so the post-war governments introduced the culture of dependency which now envelops, and in my view enslaves, a fifth of the population. The churches, and especially the Church of England – the official custodian of the nation's morals and beliefs – entered a period of steady and eventually catastrophic decline. They lost congregations but, worse, their leaders lost faith in their mission. The system of education was modernised, and huge and growing sums spent on it. Not just the religious but the moral content somehow disappeared, and with it went the discipline and the simple ethic of work which had made the old, under-endowed and dingy church schools so remarkably effective. Most people were, and still are, baffled by these changes, and unable to explain why the system, so expensive to run, seems to be failing the nation; in their disappointment and confusion they speak, vaguely, of 'a fall in standards'. At the same time as the churches and the schools were faltering, a similar transformation was begun of Britain's entire system of criminal justice, and it continues as I write. This involved a huge shift of philosophy. The object of criminal justice ceased to be primarily the protection of life and property by a system of punishment, retribution and deterrence. It began to concern itself, in the first place, with the rehabilitation of the offender and his reintegration into society from which, it was argued, he had strayed largely by misfortunes not of his making.

All these changes combined to bring about fundamental shifts in public attitudes to right and wrong. The old distinctions, which had been so clear and absolute, and were based on the Mosaic decalogue, became blurred. Society moved uneasily towards forms of moral relativism, a new dogma taught assiduously at many universities, which substituted what is done for what ought to be done. The word 'permissive' made its appearance and wormed its way into the statute book through radical 'reforms' of the law of divorce, sexual behaviour, abortion and censorship. At the same time, tremendous and in many ways welcome improvements in living standards placed ever-growing emphasis on the centrality of material pleasure in people's lives. The 'getting and spending', against which Wordsworth had warned a century and a half ago, became more and more frenzied as what had been 'the poor' ceased to be poor and acquired material possessions in an abundance hitherto denied to all but the very rich. All sought, with varying degrees of energy – or desperation – to enter the new consumers' paradise.

The result was an increase in criminal behaviour so marked and permanent as to constitute a historical event of the greatest importance. Since this growth in crime is worldwide, and found in poor as well as affluent societies – though the incidence of crime still varies greatly from one country to another – the explanation must be sought in the spirit of the times and cannot be attributed merely to the degeneration of any particular society. But in Britain (as in certain other countries, such as the Scandinavian nations) the criminalisation of a large part of society has been particularly hard to bear. The British system of justice was ancient, renowned, respected throughout the world, and remarkably effective. The courts were revered, the police admired and the small number of professional criminals held in detestation. Violence against the person was rare and large-scale social violence almost unknown. There was a tradition, more than a century old, of civil peace and honesty in central and local government, and the overwhelming majority of ordinary people identified themselves with authority, which was seen as benign. This system had survived intact, even strengthened, through all the economic vicissitudes of the 1930s.

After the war it began to collapse, and the consequences have become more obvious as each decade has passed. Crime is ubiquitous and directly affects more and more sectors of the population. Mothers are reluctant to allow their small children to play even in quiet streets. Juvenile criminality, including murder, affects the under-twelves and even the under-tens. At the other end of the age spectrum, people in their eighties and nineties, living unprotected, are savagely attacked and robbed. Women over eighty are not spared rape by brutal young thugs. Young, middle-aged and old alike find themselves victims. In a substantial street in Leeds, every single house was burgled during the period 1988–92, some several times. In 1993 alone, one in five cars in Britain was broken into. One in three women confessed they no longer liked to go out alone at night. Crime bestrides age, class, race, education, profession and district. During the period 1990–93, habitual crime ceased to be a characteristic of the inner-city areas alone, and spread even to small market towns and country districts. It is rural areas which, in the early 1990s, have registered the most rapid increase in crime. Horrifying outrages which would have seemed incredible in the 1930s are now passed over in sorrowful and shameful silence.

This sharp decline in the moral quality of life within Britain, depressing in itself, has been accompanied by a corresponding diminution of the country's place and importance in the world. The dismantling of the overseas empire began with Britain's abdication from Palestine in 1947 and continued with the end of the empire in south Asia a year later. In the late 1950s the scramble to get out of Africa began, and it was complete by the end of the 1970s. The last important colony, Hong Kong, is due to be surrendered to Communist China in 1997. Britain ceased to be a superpower in the late 1940s and by the 1990s is, at any rate in terms of economic power, ranked only fourth in the Economic Community, after Germany, France and Italy. Britain's place in the league of manufacturing and exporting states has fallen progressively. The Royal Navy ceased to be a major custodian of world peace and trade; in the 1990s it has no aircraft-carriers (the modern capital ship), merely three 'through-deck cruisers'. Britain remains a nuclear power and, on sufferance, a permanent member of the UN Security Council; but that is all. Virtually nothing else survives of the majestic power which, under Winston Churchill, fought the Second World War to a triumphant conclusion. Thus, internally and externally, the Britain I knew in my childhood had changed totally by the time, in November 1993, I began to draw my old-age pension. I doubt if many generations in the whole of history, certainly none in British history, have had to undergo such a dispiriting and humiliating experience. And that is why I have begun this tract with an autobiographical touch. To me it is a personal as well as a national tragedy. I have, along with many people of my age and older, felt this diminishing and demeaning of Britain with all my heart and soul. It has cast a long shadow over the whole of my adult life. I have never been able to reconcile myself to it, and again and again I have asked myself: why did it happen? Now I think I know the answer and will set it down. The transformation of Britain, externally and internally, was not an act of national suicide. It was never willed by the people. They took no decisions. The truth is, they were never even consulted. Democracy has failed in Britain and until it is restored to life, our national decline will continue. So: wake up Britain!

CHAPTER TWO

Throwing Away the Largest Empire in History

*T*he dismantling of the British Empire took place over a quarter of a century. It was a confused and in some ways mysterious affair. There was no master plan, no plan of any kind. One of the most momentous events in British history, in world history indeed, took place without the British Cabinet or any other body saying: 'This is our decision.' The notion that the empire was a dynamic entity, designed to bring about specific changes, rather than a permanent state, was inherent from the start. John Dee, the sixteenth-century philosopher who coined the phrase 'the British Empire' and wrote extensively about it, saw it as a means whereby the world would be civilised and Christianised. Implicit in his vision was the assumption that the process would one day be completed. By the time modern colonial administration began to emerge under the long ministry of Lord Bathurst, Secretary for the Colonies from 1812 to 1828, the idea of eventual independence as the aim of policy was beginning to take shape, though he himself never articulated it. But others, like Mountstuart Elphinstone (1779–1859), the man who replaced the old Maratha feudal empire in India by a British administration, did. He wrote of 'a moral empire', which would end once its civilising function was complete. Thomas Macaulay, who drew up the Indian law code and laid down its system of education, thought along the same lines, and so, much later in the nineteenth century, did Captain Lugard, the statesman who put together the enormous Nigerian federation, Britain's largest black African colony. The 'moral empire' concept was certainly the one I was educated to embrace.

But though the empire was conceived of as having an end, no one said when that would come. There was no timetable, even of an approximate kind. In India, the so-called Montagu Reforms, enacted in 1919, laid down the aim of eventual self-government for Britain's largest and most important possession. But the timing was left indeterminate. When Clement Attlee became Prime Minister in 1945, as head of the Labour government which was to begin the scrapping of the empire, he had certain views of his own, for he had been a member of the Simon Commission on India (1927–30) and had come to the conclusion that India should be given self-government if not outright independence sooner rather than later. But how soon? Attlee did not know. In the general election of 1945, which returned a huge Labour majority, India was hardly discussed at all. The campaign concentrated entirely on domestic issues, the unfinished war in Asia, and the speed with which de-mobilisation could take place. Years later, Attlee presented me with an inscribed copy of his little book, *From Empire to Commonwealth*, which deals with the progress of decolonisation. Nothing is said in it about consulting the British electorate to determine its wishes on the future of the empire. No such consultation took place, in 1945 or at any other time.

In fact the dismantling began almost by accident and in response to short-term pressures. The financial crisis at home was the main factor. In 1946 Britain withdrew its troops from Greece and the Aegean because it did not wish to pay for them any longer. A decision to withdraw from Egypt was taken at the same time. That left Palestine anomalously exposed and in January 1947 British service families and other civilians were evacuated, to save money and to protect them from terrorist outrages. What started as a temporary measure became permanent, and by September 1947 Britain began pulling out completely, renouncing its mandate and insisting it was going whether or not Jews and Arabs agreed to partition the state. This was an undignified scuttle, decided upon almost from day to day. It could be argued that it had the consent of the British people, at least in a negative sense, since the Jewish and Arab terrorist attacks on British troops were deeply resented by a British public which was never taught what we were supposed to be doing in Palestine in the first place. The predominant popular feeling, therefore, was that Jews and Arabs should be left to fight it out themselves. But at no stage was the electorate consulted, formally or informally. Nor did Parliament take any significant vote on the matter, merely rubber-stamping Cabinet decisions made in haste and sometimes in panic.

Meanwhile a similar process was going on in India. This was a land of hundreds of millions, and as the British administration averaged only 6000 officials and British troops about 60,000, government was obviously by consent. Lord Curzon, Viceroy at the turn of the century, described British rule in India as 'not the law of the sword but the rule of justice, bringing peace and order and good government to nearly one-fifth of the human race and holding them with so mild a restraint that the rulers are the merest handful of the ruled, a tiny speck of white foam on a dark and thunderous ocean'. Discontent with alien rule was expressed by the professional politicians of the Indian Congress and the Muslim League: they formed the 'political nation' and they were the men with whom the British government dealt, through a shared political mode of discourse. Edwin Montagu, the minister who began the independence process in 1919, put the matter bluntly. He consulted what he termed 'Indian opinion' adding, 'If we speak of "Indian opinion" we should be understood as generally referring to the majority of those who have held or are capable of holding an opinion on the matter with which we are dealing'. This 'political nation' amounted to a few tens of thousands, perhaps at most 100,000 people. The rest of the population, the 'real nation', 80 per cent of whom lived in thousands of villages rarely if ever visited by officials, was not consulted at all at any stage in the process. Whether the vast majority of the Indians, who to all appearances acquiesced in British rule, actually wished the British to stay, was not known at the time and now can never be known.

The British people played no greater part in the drama than the Indian multitudes. Most of them probably agreed with another saying of Lord Curzon's: 'As long as we rule India we are the greatest power in the world. If we lose it we shall drop straight away to a third-rate power.' Those who had actually served in India, as soldiers or civilians, were aghast at the prospect of a British evacuation which they rightly foresaw would lead to sectarian violence and slaughter on a catastrophic scale. Their views were represented by Lord Wavell, Viceroy in 1946. He was replaced by Lord Mountbatten, a liberal chosen by Mr Attlee to speed up the independence process. In fact, Mountbatten went to India on his own terms, which were that he should be allowed to determine the timetable of retreat, in conjunction with Jawaharlal Nehru, the Congress leader, and Mohammed Jinnah, head of the Muslim League. Mountbatten arrived in India on 31 March 1947. Within weeks he had decided on a partition plan, on the lines of the division of Palestine, which would enable the British to leave quickly. The Cabinet in London, with his pistol to its head, endorsed the plan on 23 May; Congress and League leaders approved it in June; and British rule legally ended on 15 August. Thus a vast empire which had grown up over three hundred years was dissolved in a few hectic weeks. The price was over three million slaughtered Indians, many of them literally torn to pieces by infuriated sectarian mobs – more by far than had been killed in the entire process of creating the empire. This slaughter was followed in turn by three wars between the two halves of the partition, India and Pakistan; by a civil war between Pakistan's two wings; and by civil strife in both India and Pakistan on a scale unknown under British dominion. So whether British withdrawal was in the interests of India's millions is an open question, and one that it is now pointless to debate. What can be said is that it was in no sense democratic. All the critical decisions seem to have been taken by three men: Mountbatten, Nehru and Jinnah. A decade later, my editor, Kingsley Martin, took me to see Jawaharlal Nehru at the Indian High Commission in London. Nehru was accompanied by his daughter, later to be Prime Minister in her turn, but then a sullen young woman. Nehru seemed to me an old man, bowed by the cares of office. I asked him what it felt like, in company with Jinnah and Mountbatten, to settle the future of so many hundreds of millions. He laughed and said, 'I'm not sure it was like that. It was all rather a muddle, really.'

The dismantling of Britain's African empire, which took place mainly in the 1960s, was more deliberative, at least in some cases. The road to independence for the Gold Coast, renamed Ghana, which was Britain's richest black colony, was carefully prepared over many years by Colonial Office bureaucrats. The same could be said for Nigeria, the largest. In both cases elaborate efforts were made to show that all the apparatus of successful self-government – political, administrative, judicial and military organisations – was in place and that local elites had been adequately trained for their new roles. It should be added, however, that there was no general British, let alone West African, participation in the independence process. On the British side, African independence was never an issue at any general election, or by-election, or the subject of public discussion. The major parties, without much enthusiasm, agreed it had to take place: was it not the spirit of the times? Debate even in Cabinet was muted. All the key decisions were taken by a handful of senior politicians and officials, urged on by a few Commonwealth correspondents and other 'experts'. On the African side, the only participants in the process were members of the 'political nation', in almost every case professional politicians who had been able to create electoral machines under Colonial Office supervision. No serious attempt was ever made to establish the views of the 'real nation', especially outside the towns. Those in charge assumed that 'the Africans' endorsed the self-interested views of their supposed political leaders, just as Cabinet ministers in Britain assumed 'the British' wanted the West African empire demolished. A few hundred people, on both sides, thus determined the futures of unconsulted millions.

Unscrambling the empire in the rest of Africa was a less considered affair, and in some cases took place without much pretence that the ex-colony was ready for self-government. On the British side, the prevailing wisdom in Whitehall was that the African colonial game was up and all that remained was to get out with dignity. Only nominal thought was given to what was likely to happen to the countless millions of largely illiterate

Africans we were leaving behind. Elaborate constitutions were, of course, drawn up; guarantees of personal rights given; parliaments established; judiciaries set up with the approval of the Inns of Court. Gradually, a routine timetable of withdrawal was worked out, culminating in a glittering signing ceremony which took place at Lancaster House in London, followed in the capital of the newly 'free' nation by a ceremonial lowering of the Union Jack attended by a minor member of the Royal Family. Thus the British elite, like Pontius Pilate, washed its hands; the African political elites, by contrast, rubbed theirs gleefully as they took possession of entire countries to command and plunder. The British electorate and the African masses were mere onlookers.

Now at the turn of the twenty-first century, the consequences of the dissolution of the British Empire, the largest in history, are displayed for all to see. India is still a democracy of a sort, though a very corrupt one, periodically shaken by civil disorder on a scale which would have been unthinkable under the British Raj. But it has a multi-party system, an independent judiciary and a free press. Pakistan oscillates between anarchic democracy, rule by family oligarchies and military dictatorship. Its dislocated east wing, Bangladesh, is an abyss of ineradicable poverty. Kashmir, the 'Garden of India', is partitioned and terrorist-ridden, most of it ruled, after a fashion, by the Indian army. The old frontier provinces of imperial India are feudal dictatorships, military colonies or areas of severe repression. Burma is one of the most savagely governed states on earth, controlled by a cruel military oligarchy. Ceylon, now Sri Lanka, is in a state of permanent civil war. Malaysia is only nominally a democracy but increasingly prosperous and apparently stable. Singapore is a strait-laced exercise in populist capitalism whose inhabitants now enjoy higher living standards than the British themselves.

The post-colonial record in Asia, therefore, is mixed, and not much remains of the liberal-democratic formulae the British sought to leave behind. In Africa, they have vanished almost without trace. All the former British colonies are now, in effect, one-party states or military dictatorships. In none of them has the rule of law survived. None has an independent judiciary, a free press, a functioning parliament or elementary free speech. Most have experienced military coups, civil and tribal wars, invasions and massacres. Some of the individual stories are pitiful. Ghana, once the richest, is now one of the poorest countries in Africa. Nigeria is a vast ruin, its fabulous oil-wealth squandered and now virtually exhausted. A particularly tragic case is Uganda, where British intervention, by ending endemic and vicious tribal warfare, had begun an epoch of unprecedented stability and prosperity. When the young Winston Churchill visited it in 1907 he was overwhelmed by its beauty and richness and by its delightful people: it was, he wrote, just as he had always imagined the country Jack discovered when he climbed to the top of the beanstalk. Uganda got its independence in 1962. Two years later the army mutinied. In 1966 what remained of democracy was abolished and in 1971, after further disasters, the country fell into the power of Idi Amin, one of the most savage rulers in Africa's history. His eight-year reign of terror, punctuated by invasion and civil war, was followed by further dictatorships, both civil and military. By the 1990s, the country was a typical African entity, riven by violent tribalism, undemocratic, corrupt and bankrupt.

Throughout north-central and east Africa, the consequences of Western withdrawal were particularly bloody and desolating. Tanzania, formerly Tanganyika, first a well-run German colony then a model British mandate, was making remarkable economic progress on the eve of independence. Once 'free', it became a one-party state of a quasi-Stalinist kind and, despite receiving more Western aid per capita than any other nation, descended into pitiful poverty. In East Africa and its Horn, Britain had heavy responsibilities, for during the years 1941–45 it had liberated the former Italian and French colonies, as well as its own, and restored the conquered throne of Ethiopia. In all these territories, independence was followed by the usual litany of horrors: coups d'état, military rule, tribal and civil war, invasion and anarchy, succeeded in turn by endemic brigandage. In large parts of this vast region, the state has ceased to exist, economic transactions are conducted at gun-point and the peasants, in despair, have left their lands and now starve in the shanty towns and refugee camps.

Perhaps the most tragic case of all is the Sudan. This had never been a colony. Since the Battle of Omdurman in 1899, it had been run jointly by Britain and Egypt as a condominium, and so successfully that it was taken as a model for the trusteeship territories created by the League of Nations after the First World War. For more than half a century, this huge expanse of desert and scrub, for the first time in its history, enjoyed peace and efficient, honest administration, conducted by a few hundred dedicated British and Egyptian expatriates, backed by less than 10,000 police and soldiers. Long before the great aid inflow of the 1950s and 1960s, such ambitious ventures as the Gezira Cotton Scheme were launched and established at tiny cost, and began to transform the economic outlook of the nomadic tribes and subsistence farmers who lived in the Upper Nile basin. People of different tribes, religions, cultural levels and racial origins lived together in harmony and growing prosperity. All this was sacrificed on the altar of nominal 'freedom'. From the late 1960s, the Sudan has experienced a fearful martyrdom of military dictatorship, civil war and one of the most ferocious religious persecutions, of Christians by Muslims, ever recorded. More than half the land once under cultivation has reverted to scrub and there are now five million peasants in camps. Millions more have been slaughtered or have died of starvation and disease.

What is so disturbing about the predicament of so many of these former colonies or protectorates is that few of the Westerners who visit them, and even fewer of those who have the misfortune to live there, can see any end to the agony. Bad, incompetent, corrupt and cruel government, or misgovernment – or no government at all – tribal anarchy, civil war, invasion and counter-invasion, agricultural distress and famine, waves of starvation, plague and endemic disease seem to be the inescapable fate of these countries for as long as anyone can foresee. It is hard to point to one, in the generation or so since independence, where *per capita* incomes have risen. In most they have fallen catastrophically. The political and military elites – successors of the men to whom Britain handed over – live in blatant luxury until their turn comes to be slaughtered. The rest, the survivors and descendants of those who were never consulted at all, are condemned to poverty and, often, sudden death. Africa has never been so dark since the first Europeans came there.

Of course the British are not alone responsible for this continental catastrophe. France, Belgium, Spain and Portugal also handed over vast territories to tiny elites who proceeded to exploit and plunder them. They too believed they were bowing to the spirit of the age. The Portuguese, to their credit, tried to fight the spirit, to the limit of their resources, but were abandoned by the rest of Europe; the only consequence of their obstinacy is that their two giant colonies, Angola and Mozambique, are perhaps the most ravaged and stricken of all. Britain, then, was not the only country to forsake the peoples it had once claimed to protect, and abandon its practical and moral responsibilities. But it was the most guilty, because its pretensions were the highest; its claims to a civilising mission the most exalted; and its success in carrying out its colonial mission increasingly marked. It possessed a large, well-trained and experienced colonial service, whose idealism and *esprit de corps* were unmatched anywhere. It had the financial and military resources to carry on. All it lacked was the will.

Yet I maintain that this collapse of will to do our duty to the Africans was not a national failure. It was a failure of the national leadership – the tiny handfuls of senior politicians, Whitehall office-holders, experts and opinion-formers who, in practice, took the decisions to abandon our charges. There was nothing democratic about it. The British people were no more consulted than the millions of hapless Africans who were thus consigned, by complacent or self-righteous or cynical power-holders in far-away London, to a future of savagery and destitution.

However, whether culpable or not, many British people certainly feel guilty about what was done, or not done. Africa is now infrequently reported by the British media – or any media. We have supped full of its horrors and want to avert our gaze. But its miseries occasionally impinge on our television screens or brush the pages of our newspapers. Then we feel guilt. I know that I do. I was the editor of a powerful journal of opinion during the 1960s, when many of the fatal moves were made, and

I know I could have done more to argue against the disreputable scuttle. There are many former colonial administrators whose own records in Africa were honourable, who feel that their work has been thrown away and shamed and who, in their retirement, follow events in the Dark Continent with an agonising mixture of sorrow, rage and pity: sorrow they were able to do so little to prevent the work of destruction, rage at those who took the decisions, and pity for the abandoned multitudes who once put their trust in us. I share these emotions, and because I share them I am determined to point out that the sacrifice of a bewildered and innocent continent to the forces of anarchy was not a national decision. It happened because democracy failed to function as it should. The lesson to be learned, and the only way in which we can express our contrition as an honourable people, is to ensure that our democracy works in future. That is the imperative: for post-war decolonisation was not the only occasion in which the ordinary people of Britain had no voice in matters of the highest concern to them. The denial of democracy has occurred, and is occurring, all the time. Let us examine more cases.

CHAPTER THREE

How the Barons Were Beaten
and What Replaced Them

One reason why Britain abandoned its responsibilities to its colonies and trusteeships was the belief of its post-war governments, well-founded or not, that it could no longer afford them. Whether the British people ever shared this conviction is not known, because they were never consulted. But it was strong among politicians, especially Labour Party politicians and most of all among the members of the Attlee Cabinet, 1945–51. These men were baffled by the problems confronting them when they took office during the closing stages of the war. The peace brought no respite and their pessimism and defeatism came to a climax during the fearful winter of 1946–7, when months of freezing weather exhausted available fuel supplies and brought British industry to a virtual standstill. It was during this period of panic on the part of Cabinet ministers that the scuttle in Palestine and the rapid partition of and withdrawal from India – the hasty beginnings of decolonisation – were determined.

How strong was Britain? How weak was Britain? There are no objective answers to these questions, then or now. In the last resort, a nation is as strong as its people believe it to be and will it to be. But if its governing elite is dejected and demoralised, and if its democratic machinery functions so badly that the people cannot make their voice heard, then it will seem weak and continue to be weak. The British are, by any standards, a remarkable people. As John Milton, in his majestic address to Parliament, pleading for freedom of publication, put it:

Lords and Commons of England! – Consider what nation it is whereof you are and of which you are the Governors: a nation not slow or dull, but of quick, ingenious and piercing spirit; acute to invent, subtile and sinewy to discourse, not beneath the reach of any point that human capacity can soar to.

In the quarter-century from 1760, the British were the first to industrialise themselves, the first to achieve, as a nation, lift-off into self-sustaining economic growth. For most of the nineteenth century, a majority of the world's trade in manufactures was conducted from Britain, with British goods, carried in British ships. Until 1914 and in some respects well beyond, London was the financial and economic captial of the world and Britain the heart of the international capitalist system.

Yet Britain and the British had and have a weakness: an excessive liberalism, a misguided over-tolerance, an unwillingness to use the knife and carry out the needful surgery on the body politic. Of course this weakness has its advantages. It makes Britain in many ways the most agreeable country in which to live. It ensures a high degree of civil peace and constitutional continuity. In the two centuries since industrialisation, Britain is the only major industrial power which has not suffered the convulsions of revolution, foreign conquest or civil war. These fundamental breaks with the past are ugly and usually violent – often horrifically so. They scar and coarsen the national psyche, with unpredictable results. But they also promote social and economic dynamism. In the nineteenth and twentieth centuries Britain fought its wars abroad, and long domestic tranquillity softened its competitive spirit and its ferocious native will to excel.

Nor was this all, alas. Liberalism, with its overweening desire to be fair, even or rather especially to the weak, often results in huge and baleful misjudgements, which incur heavy penalties. Britain's early and successful industrialisation was made possible by its liberal and comparatively efficient legal framework, which allowed the pioneering entrepreneurs an astonishing amount of freedom. Britain had no written constitution with individual rights graven in legal granite. But it had a body of statute law going back to Magna Carta, which has headed the statute book since 1215; and, more important still, it had and has a living Common Law, arbitrated by judges, which effectively upholds rights of liberty and property. It was precisely the broadmindedness and flexibility of this Common Law tradition which enabled the first modern industrial society to emerge. Throughout the nineteenth century it continued to function as an effective legal setting for industrial enterprise.

But industrialisation, thanks to our excessive liberalism, brought a challenge to the Common Law, initially insignificant, in time almost fatal. Trade unions – that is, combinations of workers formed to promote their specific interests – existed in England from at least the 1660s, in the mining districts of the northeast and the ports which handled 'sea coal'. They were abhorrent to the Common Law for two reasons: first, they militated against its fundamental doctrine of equality before the law, because a union by seeking exclusive advantages for its members automatically threatened the lawful rights of others; and second, because a union by its very nature sought to secure its objects by duress and force rather than through the courts. So far as the records allow us to judge, the use and threat of force to compel workers to join was a characteristic of British trade unions, especially in the coalfields and ports, from their very origins. The 'closed shop' is a very ancient British institution. Moreover, force or the threat of it was also regularly employed to compel reluctant or unwilling workers to take part in strikes, boycotts and even violence. Because unions exist to secure workers' rights, it is a mistake to assume they are democratic institutions, or ever have been. They are blunt instruments, which cannot afford the niceties of democratic debate, hesitation and division. They are almost invariably run by men of fundamentalist views, who believe the honourable end justifies the often dishonourable means, and who bring a tunnel vision to public life in which trade union rights have moral precedence over any others. The earliest union rulebooks were carefully designed to enable the fundamentalists, constituting majorities which were far more notional than real, to oppress the rest.

When liberal-minded British statesmen, anxious to mitigate the manifest evils of industrialisation by making concessions to the workers, began to enshrine the privileges unions demanded in statute law, at the expense of the Common Law, they quickly discovered the propensity of trade union leaders to exploit any legal advantages which came their way by employing coercion. The first trade union rights bill, enacted by Sir Robert Peel, Home Secretary, in 1824, led to so much union violence, including murder, that he was forced to re-enact it the following year, giving elementary protection to workers who refused to obey union leaders.

Despite this disillusioning experience, British politicians, both Tory and Liberal, continued from time to time to give unions, as corporate bodies, legal privileges denied to everyone else. Thus in 1871 Gladstone gave them special legal status which enabled them to protect their funds in ways denied to their opponents, industrial enterprises. In 1875, Disraeli passed the Conspiracy and Protection of Property Act, which made lawful the unions' favourite form of intimidation, known as 'peaceful picketing'. The courts did their best to protect individuals or bodies harmed by these special privileges by using the resources of the Common Law. Thus in 1901, in the Taff Vale judgment, the courts qualified the 1871 Act by establishing the principle that unions, when they behaved unlawfully, could be sued for damages.

It was this key judgment which detonated the long and tragic history of modern trade unionism in Britain. The British of all classes are reasonable people, and there was no inherent reason why the legitimate interests of those who belong to unions should not be fairly and peacefully reconciled with those of all other members of society. And so they would have been, had the burgeoning British democracy functioned properly. But it was not to be. In 1900 the unions, organised in the Trades Union Congress, created the Labour Party, specifically to promote sectional legislation creating legal privileges or, as its constitution put it, 'legislation in the direct interest of labour', and to oppose 'measures having an opposite tendency'. The salient characteristic of the Labour Party, therefore, was that unlike other socialist movements on the Continent or even in the United States, it was not Marxist or even socialist as such, but a form of parliamentary syndicalism. That did not make it democratic; quite the contrary. The unions directly sponsored a hard core of Labour Members of Parliament (128 in 1975, for instance) and, more important, paid about 75 per cent of the party's national funds and 95 per cent of its election expenses. In return, the unions became the overwhelmingly dominant element in the formation of party policy – and thus in the conduct of a Labour government, once elected – by a system known as the 'block vote' at party conferences. The size of the block vote was determined not by the number of members the union possessed, nor even by the percentage of them who wished to belong to the Labour Party, but by the size of the affiliation fee each union leadership passed over to the party's coffers. This iniquitous system placed enormous power in the hands of individual trade union leaders, who thus became 'barons', and who eventually cast the votes, at their own whim or will, of millions of nominal members. Despite its un-democratic nature, which effectively undermines the claim of Labour to be a democratic party, the block vote persists to this day.

The block vote apparatus became the means by which a huge pyramid of trade union statutory privileges was progressively assembled. In 1906, for the first time, more than fifty Labour MPs were returned to Parliament, and their bargaining power with the Liberal government was such that it passed the Trade Disputes Act (1906), which reversed the Taff Vale judgment and gave unions complete immunity from civil actions for damages (torts) 'alleged to have been committed by and on behalf of the trade unions'. Such immunity existed nowhere else in the civilised West, for in effect it made unions impervious to actions for breach of contract, though other parties to the contract, the employers, could still be sued by the unions. As the great constitutional lawyer, A. V. Dicey, protested at the time: 'It makes a trade union a privileged body exempted from the ordinary laws of the land. No such privileged body has ever before been deliberately created by an English parliament.'

But this was only the plinth of the pyramid. The Trade Union Act of 1913 legalised the spending of union funds on political objectives, i.e. the Labour Party, and, further, forced union members who supported other parties to 'contract out' of this subscription, a process deliberately made difficult and unpopular and subject to intimidation. This odiously un-democratic procedure, which in effect obliged hundreds of thousands, perhaps millions, of working men and women to support financially a particular political party, was so unpopular that in 1927, following the collapse of the General Strike, a Tory government plucked up the courage to reverse it, and substitute 'contracting in'.

However, the 1927 statute and all other legal enactments to protect the public, and individual union members, from the tyranny of the barons, was swept away when a Labour government was returned in strength in 1945. The electorate voted in large numbers for a better life for the ordinary working people of Britain. That was a democratic decision. What they got, in practice, was nationalisation of industry, placing power over huge sectors of the economy in the hands of oligarchies appointed by union leaders and government, and further union privileges. The Labour government, under orders, gave the unions special status within the nationalised industries it had created, and indeed within all its social and economic policy legislation. The judges continued, from time to time, to uphold the protection traditionally given by the Common Law to weak individuals oppressed by large corporations, such as unions. But whenever judges found a hole in trade union privilege law, the unions were able to lean directly on a Labour-dominated Parliament to plug it. Thus in 1964 the Law Lords, in *Rookes v. Barnard*, held that an unofficial strike – that is, one called by extremists without going through the usual union rulebook procedures – was actionable if in breach of contract. The next year, a new Labour government legalised this monstrous abuse by pushing through the 1965 Trade Disputes Act.

During the 1960s and 1970s, the power of the unions, or rather of the union barons and the militant elites which kept them in place, became ever more strident and undemocratic. In 1969, the union leaders vetoed the so-called 'In Place of Strife' legislation, introduced by the Labour Prime Minister, Harold Wilson, to reduce the number of damaging strikes; that, in effect, was the end of his government. In 1972, union leaders introduced new forms of what they called 'direct action' (i.e. organised violence), in the shape of 'mass picketing', 'flying pickets' and 'secondary picketing', which the police were unable or unwilling to curb. In effect these devices, which were completely alien to the Common Law, were simply a way of allowing militant union leaders to switch mobs of men, often armed, from one part of the country to another, to achieve whatever ends they thought fit. In 1974 these devices were used to destroy a Conservative government responsible for the 1971 Industrial Relations Act which attempted, albeit ineffectually, to introduce a statutory code of union conduct.

The Labour government which was thus brought to power in 1974 not only repealed the 1971 Act but pushed through Parliament a mass of legislation extending union privileges still further. Of this, the Trade Union and Labour Relations Acts of 1974 and 1976, and the Employment Protection Acts of 1975 and 1979, were merely the most important. Much of this legislation the union barons were invited to write themselves, and supply to the government in draft form. It would be difficult to conceive of a more illiberal code than the one which thus emerged, contrary not only to all our ancient libertarian traditions but to the basic principles of natural law. The new code extended immunity in tort actions to cases where unions induced (i.e. forced) other parties to break contracts, obliged employers to recognise unions and uphold 'closed shops' (to the point where a worker could be dismissed without legal remedy for refusing to join a union) and to provide facilities for union organisation. The effect of the code was greatly to increase the number of 'closed shop' industries and to push unionisation above the 50-per-cent mark of the workforce for the first time in history (compared with 25 per cent or less in the United States, France and Germany, for instance). Even more important, however, it removed virtually all legal inhibitions on the power of the barons. As the Master of the Rolls, Lord Denning, sorrowfully observed: 'All legal restraints have been lifted so that they can now do as they will.'

What were the economic consequences of this terrifying and cumulative growth in union legal power? They are worth examining in a little detail because of their immense long-term effect on the position of Britain in the world and their impact on British society even today. Unions acted as a brake on British economic dynamism as early as the 1820s. It is possible to build up an overwhelming case against them entirely on nineteenth-century and early twentieth-century evidence, particularly in certain key industries. But it was only after the legislative changes of the late 1940s that the unions began to inflict critical damage over the whole spectrum of the British economy. The figures soon spoke for themselves. In 1950 the British gross national product was $47 billion; the combined figure for its six continental neighbours (France, Italy, Germany, Belgium, the Netherlands and Luxembourg) who formed the original European Community, was $75 billion. British exports, at $6.3 billion, were more than two-thirds those of the Six, and GNP per capita, at $940, was nearly twice as high. Twenty years later, in 1970, British GNP per capita had more than doubled, to $2170. That of the Six had multiplied more than five times, to $2557. While British exports had tripled, those of the Six had multiplied nearly ten times. Their reserves, smaller than Britain's in 1950, had multiplied by ten, whereas Britain's had declined. By any possible measurement, the British economy had performed badly in comparison with those of its nearest neighbours. Membership of the European Community was not the reason, or at any rate not the main reason, that the gap in performance widened in the 1970s, despite the fact that Britain actually joined the EEC on 1 January 1973. The main reason was British trade union privilege law.

Excessive union power contributed to the slowness of Britain's growth mainly in three ways. First, it promoted restrictive practices, inhibited the growth of productivity and so discouraged investment. In the quarter-century 1950–75, Britain's investment and productivity record was the worst of any major industrial power. Second, it greatly increased the pressure of wage inflation, especially from the late 1960s onwards. Third, trade union social and legislative demands on government had a cumulative tendency to increase the size of the public-sector and government share of GNP. Britain had traditionally been a minimum-government state. That was why it had become first free, then rich. As Thomas Hobbes, our most perceptive political philosopher, neatly put it: 'The freedom of the subject is the silence of the laws.' The silence of the laws and the inactivity of the state formed the benevolent framework within which the industrial revolution occurred. The Census of 1851 registered less than 75,000 civil public employees, mostly customs, excise and postal workers, with only 1628 manning the central departments of civil government, at a time when the corresponding figure for France (1846) was 932,000!

In the century that followed, the proportion of the working population employed in the public sector rose gradually from 2.4 per cent to 24.3 per cent in 1950, by which date the Labour government was nationalising industry and expanding the welfare state as fast as it could. During the 120 years 1790–1910, when Britain was paramount in the world economy, the proportion of its GNP accounted for by public expenditure never rose over 23 per cent and averaged 13 per cent. After 1946 it never fell below 36 per cent. In 1965 it passed 45 per cent and in 1967 50 per cent. The 55-per-cent mark was passed just after Labour returned to office in 1974. In 1975–6 public-sector borrowing alone had reached 11.5 per cent of total output and the aggregate of public borrowing over the past five years alone exceeded £31 billion. By this point the combination of public borrowing and wage inflation threatened to push Britain's inflation rate over the 40-per-cent band. In the autumn of 1976 the Labour government was obliged to call in the broker's men of the International Monetary Fund and submit to their diktat. Such a humiliation had never before occurred in British history.

Though the damage inflicted by union power on the British economy as a whole was incalculable, in particular industries it was horribly specific. In the docks, for instance, London was forced to surrender its proud place as Europe's busiest port to Rotterdam. Other great ports like Liverpool suffered correspondingly, as a result of a union-dictated institution known as the Dock Labour Scheme, under which 'registered dockers', that is those who belonged to the union closed shop, were guaranteed jobs for life, whether or not there was any work for them to do. Many ports virtually closed down: only those too small to belong to the scheme flourished. The effect of the scheme was not only to destroy Britain's entrepot trade but to inflict huge damage on the export trade too.

In printing, where the unions exercised more power than in any other industry and the closed shop was universal, union members not only had jobs for life but were paid for jobs which did not exist. At the apogee of union power, in the 1970s, there were thousands of 'ghost workers' in the British national newspaper industry, drawing immense weekly salaries, on which they paid no tax, for entirely notional work. At the same time, a multitude of restrictive practices, known in the trade as 'old Spanish customs', not only prevented the introduction of new technology but in effect inhibited management from managing at all. The result was the death of many fine newspapers and magazines and the editorial starvation of others. British newspaper bureaux were closed down all over the world so that 'ghost workers' might thrive. As inevitably happens in cases where powerful men get above the law, corruption thrived too: the industry was rotten with bribery and underhand payments from top to bottom. In Fleet Street, which should by the mid-1970s have modernised itself into the electronic age, the stench of greed and chicanery was even stronger than the rank smell of old-fashioned printer's ink. To please Harold Wilson, I had agreed in 1975 to serve on a Royal Commission formed to inquire into the state of the press and try to improve it. It was a waste of time. At every stage, the unions prevented the Commission from making its necessary inquiries, even threatening to shut down newspapers, and by their presence within the Commission they effectively vetoed any damaging criticisms. At this time, moreover, the print unions began to employ their power to censor the press itself, so that newspapers sometimes appeared with blank spaces where compositors had declined to set copy criticising union actions. There were moments, indeed, when I felt I might just as well be living in the Soviet Union.

Union power, in the shape of the Amalgamated Engineering Union and similar bodies which led a parasitical existence on the back of industry, had a devastating effect between 1945 and

1980 on the West Midlands, the heart of British manufacturing, and especially on the car industry. At the end of the war the British car industry was the second largest in the world after the giants of Detroit. By the end of the 1970s it had been almost destroyed. The managing director of one of the largest British motor manufacturers, which no longer exists, told me that each year he had to take part in no less than 365 separate union negotiations, one for each day: 'When do I get time to manage, even if I were allowed to do such a thing?'

When I think of those dead firms, killed by union extremists, firms which in many cases went back to the very origins of motorcars and had produced some of the finest talents in the history of engineering, my memory conjures up the smiling, silly features and the flat, comical Manchester voice of Hugh Scanlon, president of the AEU during the critical years 1968–78, a job which crowned a lifetime of agitation in the industry. On various occasions I debated with Scanlon on television and found him a likeable fellow. Supremely foolish he was, because his activities, undertaken supposedly in the interests of his members, ended often enough by destroying their jobs. But he meant no harm. There was no evil in him. To this day – and at the time of writing he is still with us – he is probably quite unaware of the mischief he and his kind created for our industry. The evil lay not in him, but in an iniquitous system which placed so much destructive power in the hands of men such as he, the baronage. In due course, like so many of his colleagues – some of whom were indeed evil men – he became a real baron, for one of James Callaghan's last acts as Prime Minister was to make Scanlon a life peer. What, I wonder, for: helping to destroy the British motorcar industry?

From 1968–9 onwards, when I first encouraged Barbara Castle and Harold Wilson to legislate to knock the union juggernaut off its rails – then, like them, watched impotently as the barons terrified the Cabinet and the Parliamentary Labour Party into dropping the scheme – I became convinced that the emasculation of the unions was priority number one if the British people were to have an honourable and prosperous future. I was told, time and time again, not just by the trade unions barons themselves but by politicians of all parties, media and academic experts and discouraged ordinary people, that it was simply not possible to subject the unions to what I regarded as the necessary legal restraints. Throughout the 1970s, this was the view of the overwhelming majority of people in public life. Needless to say, this was the line of the Labour Party leadership: having burnt their fingers once, they were not going to take on the union bosses again. That was why I left the Labour Party in the mid-1970s, and why I threw in my lot with Margaret Thatcher, the new leader of the Conservatives, when she swore to me – 'Cross my heart and hope to die' were her words – that, come what may, she would bring the unions back within the law.

As it turned out, the union barons played straight into her resolute hands. The episode was rich in irony. No Labour politician had done more to advance the pretensions of the unions than Jim Callaghan, Prime Minister from 1976 to 1979. They had helped him by pushing him to the top of the party and he, in turn, had done their business at every stage of his tortuous career. It was he who in 1969 had conspired, behind the backs of his Cabinet colleagues, to upset the In Place of Strife policy – as any reader of Richard Crossman's *Cabinet Diaries* will know – and who, the moment he became Prime Minister, had exacted the barons' revenge and ended Barbara Castle's career at a stroke. As head of the government, no one was more assiduous than Callaghan in serving union interests. However, Almighty God, in his infinite wisdom, made them stupid. Their stupidity compelled them not merely to undermine the long-term interests of their members – they had always done that – but on this occasion to act directly contrary to their own. In 1978–9 they launched, not according to any deep-laid plan but in the intoxication of their own overweening power, a series of strikes which inflicted harm on almost every aspect of British life – even the dead, who went unburied – and caused the nation to call the season 'the Winter of Discontent'. Callaghan commanded them to desist; then coaxed, whined, pleaded, went down on his knees to the baronage, alternately cursing them and begging them to stop. By this stage however, the barons were no longer in control of their own cavalry, who pillaged and looted at will. The Prime Minister, thus betrayed by the very men he had devoted his life to serving, found his electoral time running out, and in May 1979 was forced to go before an angry nation, which disgustedly tipped him into the dustbin of history and replaced the lid. Margaret Thatcher got exactly the mandate she desired.

She had also learned a valuable lesson from the sad history of the all-embracing 1971 Industrial Relations Act, a complex and highly legalistic document which tried to solve all the problems of trade unionism in one go and failed miserably. Rejecting this approach, she set about the problem on a step-by-step basis, enacting in all five separate Acts over the space of three parliaments. These progressively ended a whole series of special legal privileges enjoyed by unions, made many strikes and forms of picketing unlawful, and subjected unions that broke the law to severe financial penalties. Mrs Thatcher also made it clear that the police, in dealing with 'mass', 'flying' and 'secondary' pickets, which had made it virtually impossible in the 1970s for employers to resist wage demands backed by strikes, and so inflicted grievous damage on both the private and public sectors, would be fully backed by her government. Thus reassured, individual police forces recast their tactics and formed a nationwide strategy to meet the threat of unlawful picketing.

How long the new legislation would have taken to master the trade union menace if left entirely to the courts it is hard to judge. As it happened, its impact was greatly accelerated, and reinforced, by the decision of both the miners' leaders and the print-workers' leaders to use the brute power of some of Britain's strongest closed-shop unions to break the new laws by force. This was trade union 'direct action' – in effect industrial warfare – on a spectacular scale, leading in both cases to total defeat. Here is not the place to recall in detail the course of the Scargill coal strike of 1984–5 or the Wapping print strike of 1986. In both cases the combination of law, well-organised policing and (in consequence) a new resolution of management proved too strong even for the ruthlessly led and highly disciplined unions. In both cases the unions involved were permanently emasculated and their leaders humiliated. The human and financial costs were enormous. The coal strike appears to have cost the country, in total, over £7 billion. Five people were killed and 2740 strikers convicted of various offences; 700 were sacked for 'gross industrial misconduct' and 30,000 lost their jobs. The National Union of Mineworkers, once the Brigade of Guards of British trade unionism, was financially ruined, severed into two parts and reduced by two-thirds. It is an illustration of the almost complete lack of democracy of British trade unionism that this calamitous strike was decided upon by a tiny elite of militants led by the union's president-for-life, Arthur Scargill. I debated with Scargill a number of times on television and felt a chill whenever I found myself in the same room with him. He is the most destructive creature I have ever met, impervious to objective fact or to any truth except as revealed to him, with all the granitic self-righteousness of a false messiah. Democracy meant nothing to him. At no time were the ordinary members of the union allowed to vote on whether they wanted a strike or not and there is good reason to suppose that, if so allowed, they would have voted heavily against it. Yet it was the ordinary miners who lost jobs, savings, health and in some cases their lives. And it was their disastrous and destructive general, Scargill, who kept his job.

The coal strike left nothing but ruin in its wake, inflicting lasting and perhaps terminal damage on the British coal industry, once the greatest in the world. The Wapping print strike, on the other hand, though conducted with equal savagery, had positive results. By breaking the power of the print unions, the strongest and greediest in Britain, it turned the national newspaper industry almost overnight from an ailing and demoralised sector into one of the healthiest and most profitable in the economy. Vast investment schemes immediately became possible and were carried through. From being technologically one of the most backward in the West, British newspapers became among the most modern and enterprising. New papers were created; old ones hugely expanded. All became larger and better printed. Higher historic standards of foreign news coverage were gradually restored. Many more journalistic jobs were created and journalistic wage-rates improved notably. The spin-off in the provincial press, the magazine world, and the media generally – including television and cable – was incalculable.

Moreover, it was the defeat of the printers at Wapping which finally convinced the remaining unions that the game was up. Thereafter, they have obeyed the new laws, and Britain has entered into a period of industrial peace of a kind unknown for many decades. By the early 1990s, Britain's strike record, having been the worst, had become the best in the advanced industrial world. It is an amazing reversal and undoubtedly one which had the democratic approval of the nation. Virtually all the new laws were approved by the union rank-and-file, and many even by union leaders; most were eventually accepted, in one form or another, by the Labour Party. The public as a whole endorsed them wholeheartedly, and workers generally showed their support with their feet; now they were free to do so, they left the unions in large numbers, reducing total union membership by more than a third. The effect on the economy has been in some respects spectacular. In the decade 1983–93, and especially towards the end of it, British productivity gains were among the highest in the world, and probably the highest in its entire industrial history. Throughout the private sector, at least, management are able to manage again and firms to conduct long-term investment plans in the reasonable certitude that the workforce will cooperate to make them successful. For that reason Britain has become, for the first time in its history, a magnet for foreign industrial investment.

However, that is not the end of Britain's union problem, unfortunately. By the mid-1990s it has been largely mastered in the private sector. But in the public sector unions such as Nalgo, Cohse and Nupe (now united) continue to exact their toll on the economy in the form of overmanning, restrictive practices and gross inefficiency. One legacy of successive Labour governments is that unions which operate in the public sector enjoy extraordinary extra-legal privileges and negotiating rights. It is the built-in power of the two chief rail unions, the NUR and Aslef, for instance, which lies at the root of the continuing difficulties and poor service of both British Rail and London Underground. These two publicly-owned networks continue to lag behind their counterparts on the European continent, whereas British Airways and British Steel, which were privatised in the 1980s, were able to reach sensible deals with their respective unions and rapidly became European leaders. In the 1980s, British Steel became for a time the world's most profitable steel company and British Airways became and remained highly profitable at a time when most other major airlines were losing money. As nationalised concerns in the 1970s, both had registered some of the highest corporate losses in history.

This turnabout has been so extraordinary, and the lessons arising from it so plain, that it is hard to comprehend why the national and London rail networks are not privatised with all possible speed, or why the public-sector unions should not be made subject to the same laws as private-sector unions. Yet it is a curious fact that those who complain loudest about their unarguable shortcomings are most determined to retain the status quo: their only solution, in both cases, is a huge increase in investment. Experience has shown time and again that hurling taxpayers' money at nationalised industries where unions are still strong and privileged actually makes matters worse. Most of it goes immediately on higher wages, shorter hours and more restrictive practices. The net result is to demoralise management still further, for even the residue which does go directly into investment has to be spent according to the notions of the union barons.

The futility of increasing spending without changing the structure and climate of the public sector has been shown repeatedly in local government and the National Health Service. These two enormous concerns were virtually untouched by the Thatcher reforms. They both employ vast numbers of people, some abysmally badly paid, some surprisingly well paid, and both for reasons which have little or nothing to do with productivity or the services they render. Both are heavily unionised, often in closed shops, and are carved up between the giant public-sector unions and smaller bodies. The National Health Service, with well over a million workers, is easily the largest employer in Europe and almost certainly among the least efficient, with many more service staff than doctors and nurses. Local government, though varying greatly from place to place, is in general an abyss of petty bureaucracy and sheer incompetence, with a few officials grossly overworked and many more almost entirely idle, and with all the evils that go with such a system – excessive paperwork and absurd regulations, corruption, absenteeism and internal vendettas.

The cost of these two institutions almost beggars belief. In 1994 we are spending £29,920 million on local government from central funds, quite apart from what we have to pay in council tax. Most of this goes in wages and salaries. It is the same story in the NHS, which is costing even more: £31,730 million in 1994. Again, most of this immense sum goes into paying employees. We have learned repeatedly that overmanning is almost invariably an obstacle to efficiency. Lord King cut British Airways' workforce by half and simultaneously transformed the company for the better; Air France, which retains the old inflated levels, enjoys in consequence all the misfortunes of strikes, cancellations, bad temper, poor morale and losses which, in 1993–4, are expected to exceed £1 billion. All the available evidence suggests that if the NHS workforce were cut from one-million-plus to 500,000, the British people would enjoy far better health care. Yet in this case, the obduracy and power of the unions are reinforced by public sentiment which continues to treat this discredited concern as a sacred cow, too precious to be touched.

We have here, again, a problem in democracy. During the 1980s, Mrs Thatcher and her colleagues, like Norman Tebbit, were able to mobilise public opinion behind a frontal assault on the thoroughly undemocratic institution of lawless trade unionism. Properly led, as they were in this case, the British people displayed admirable qualities of common sense, courage and enthusiasm. The result was a famous victory and a huge improvement in the performance of the private sector – as well as a freeing of the nation from the tyranny of strikes, go-slows, work-to-rules and union-led violence. But similar leadership has been absent in dealing with the equally serious problems of the remaining public sector. And, with leadership lacking, there has been no public response. So democracy has failed to work. Can we learn this lesson too?

We must also learn that it is no use freeing British industry and services from the slavery of restrictions and inhibitions imposed by the union barons if we replace these shackles by others forged by government. Yet that is precisely what has happened and is happening. And therein lies a mystery. One of Margaret Thatcher's fundamental objects was to free British enterprise from excessive government. That was a noble and sensible aim and one shared by the overwhelming majority of the British people. It was a democratic aim, democratically endorsed. The highly successful privatisation programme was an important part of this aim. Now here we come to the irony. At exactly the same time as huge chunks of the nationalised sector were being freed from bureaucratic rule and returned to the entrepreneurs and the market, massive parliamentary statutes were being passed to increase government regulations of every kind. The longer Mrs Thatcher held power, the more numerous and oppressive these laws became. Some of them began in response to popular criticism, but they rapidly turned into legislative monsters. First came the Data Protection Act of 1984, a Byzantine catalogue of dos and don'ts. Then in 1986 there was the mind-boggling Financial Services Act, a lawyer's paradise and a businessman's nightmare, which has been greeted by professional City slickers and outright crooks with incredulous laughter, and by honest men and women with total dismay. In 1988 we had the Educational Reform Act, a mass of infuriating and damaging diktats. In 1989 followed the already notorious Children's Act, a large-scale frontal assault on common sense, Christian morality and the family, which has all kinds of horrifying implications for industry. The year 1990 – Mrs Thatcher's last, as it happened – was an *annus mirabilis* of reglementation: the Care of the Countryside Act, a new Health and Safety Act and the Environmental Protection Act. This statutory trio imposed literally thousands of new duties, inhibitions and restrictions on industry, agriculture, services of every kind and the ordinary public. Some of the most onerous of them have yet to come into force and their reverberations will echo through the rest of the decade.

In combination, these statutes create a new penal code for Britain, substituting for the tyranny of the unions the despotism of brand-new inspectorates, field-grey regiments of intrusive quasi-policemen, often working in secret and usually paid by results – the more regulations enforced and the more convictions secured, the higher their pay. So far as I can discover, the impulse behind every one of these oppressive new statutes was a small but highly active and vocal specialist lobby, representing no one but themselves, but working skilfully with civil servants whose own powers and prospects are advanced by getting this legislation through Parliament. Responsible ministers played comparatively little part in this process; MPs, except when themselves attached to (and in some cases paid by) lobbies, virtually none at all. At no point was the public as a whole – the electorate – consulted. Their views were not sought, their approval was not secured. The statutory and reglementary inflation of the late 1980s was a copybook exercise in the denial of democracy.

On top of this, and compounding it, is the horrifying story of Britain's relationship with the European Union. That is another exercise in democracy-denial and it is worth a separate chapter.

CHAPTER FOUR

Handing Brussels Britain on a Plate

*T*he story of the emergence of the European Union, and of Britain's relationship with it, is a strange one, composed almost equally of idealism and altruism on the one hand and of greed, treachery and deceit on the other, the whole compounded by stupidity and bungling on a colossal scale. And there is an ironic twist, which is directly relevant to the theme of this latter-day pamphlet. Though all the nations which took part in this tale are nominally democracies, the story which unfolded was at no point whatever determined by democratic choice. All was done by élites. The people never came into it.

When I left the British army at the end of 1951 I determined to complete my education by spending some time in Paris and was lucky enough to secure, as my first job, an editorial post with the French magazine *Réalités*. This remarkable monthly had been founded by a group of young war veterans and resistance fighters who swore that the fatal conjunction of weakness and drift which brought France so low in 1940 and led to all the humiliations and horror of the Vichy régime should never recur. They wanted France to be strong but they wanted it to be so not in solitary grandeur – that was the idea of General de Gaulle, whom they discounted as *ancien régime* – but as an integrated part of a European union, which itself would be the eastern arm of the Atlantic Alliance.

The most striking fact about the journalists and politicians associated with *Réalités* was their cosmopolitanism. The first and most important item on their agenda was a total French reconciliation with Germany, which they saw as the only guarantee of France's security and the future peace of Europe. But almost equally desirable, in their minds, was the closest possible association between France and the Anglo-American nexus. When referring to us and the Americans they did not use de Gaulle's slightly contemptuous and even racist term, *les Anglo-Saxons*. They called us 'the English-speaking allies'. Most of them spoke English fluently and were well-read in British and American literature and history. Unlike de Gaulle and his followers – unlike, indeed, a large number of ordinary Frenchmen – they had no trace of Anglophobia or anti-Americanism.

This group included prominent politicians, like for instance René Pleven, for a time Prime Minister and veteran of many Cabinets. But the most influential, the central figure in fact, was Jean Monnet. Monnet is rightly recognised as the 'onlie begetter' of the European Union, the architect whose energy, ingenuity and vision made a united Europe possible. But he was much more than that. He was a truly international, indeed global, statesman. He came from a family of Cognac producers exporting all over the world, and from the age of sixteen he was in business abroad, usually as a merchant banker or negotiating state loans. In the First World War he was in the office of Etienne Clementel, Minister of Commerce, the first Frenchman to believe that government and capitalist enterprise should work closely together to promote the common welfare, and that 'the democratic peoples', by which he meant Western Europe and the United States and Canada, should form an 'economic union'. Monnet's training was thus of the best, and in the Second World War he performed outstanding services, mainly in Washington and London, in coordinating Allied war production.

Monnet believed profoundly in his dream of a united Europe, and he had all the great French virtues of logic, orderliness and clarity. But he was a citizen of the English-speaking world too, and admired its qualities: the love of freedom, the genius for parliamentary government, the liberal spirit of trade and the distrust of over-centralisation and bureaucracy. Unusually for a Frenchman who spent most of his life in or dealing with government, he had none of the Napoleonic conviction that the state should do all. He feared the state as not only oppressive but inefficient, and he sought to keep it small. Like his mentor Clementel he wanted an emergent Europe to have an organic relationship with North America; and, failing this, he determined to construct it in such a way that the fundamental interests of Europe and North America should always be in close harmony. This meant that Britain, a country he loved, should be closely associated with Europe at every stage and that British political traditions should infuse its structures. That, in turn, meant a Europe based upon the principle of 'voluntarism'. The individual states composing Europe, and its executive authority, should not command but invite, counsel, persuade and encourage. He called this 'indicative planning', as opposed to the hateful 'command economy' of the Soviet system. He spoke of '*l'Europe des amis*'. He had his own version of Parkinson's Law, which had not yet been formulated: 'Regulations increase in accordance with the number of officials available to formulate them.' He hated bureaucracy, and the planning agencies he set up first for France itself, and then for the European Coal–Steel Pool, were notably small by Continental standards. I recall him saying, 'I need just a few people – but they must be good.' He looked for qualities of pragmatism, tolerance and breadth of view, qualities he associated particularly with the British.

Needless to say, the failure of Britain to participate, right from the start, in the building of Europe was a personal tragedy for Monnet, as well as an international tragedy for everyone else. How did this come about? One thing is certain: it was not through any wish of the British people. There was nothing democratic about this lost opportunity. In the immediate post-war years, when I was an adolescent and a young man, I recall that the prevailing British view towards Western Europe was warm, concerned and anxious. We had been through a hard war but we realised that the sufferings of the French, Belgians, Dutch and others had been infinitely greater than ours and we wanted to help them rebuild their shattered countries. The respect accorded to Britain in Europe at that time was enormous. Britain was regarded as a sanctuary of freedom and justice, and her people as one who, in the darkest days, had kept burning the sacred flame of democracy and decency. We reciprocated this good feeling and were keen to give it further substance by finding ways of binding Europe together in such a way that the menace of German hegemony would never return.

That was the general feeling of the British people, I am sure. But, in the art of government, there is a particular problem in translating popular wishes into foreign policy. The instinct of the rulers is to regard such wishes as highly dangerous. Foreign policy, they think, is a matter for the informed few, the experienced and wise elect, who see all, know all and decide all. Queen Elizabeth I, that great European stateswoman, called such matters 'the arcana of power', to be settled well away from the public gaze. There were some secrets she refused to share even with her ministers, and others she discussed at dead of night, the candles flickering in her closet, with Lord Burghley or Sir Francis Walsingham alone. This practice of secrecy persisted into the age of parliamentary democracy. Gladstone had the Cabinet tables so arranged that he and his Foreign Secretary sat together at an angle to the rest of their colleagues, emphasising the distinction between domestic affairs, the concern of all, and foreign matters, in which the part of the others was secondary. On repeated occasions in the last two hundred years, important decisions on defence and foreign policy have been kept secret not only from the public and Parliament but from most members of the Cabinet. Thus in the events leading up to the First World War, the exact nature of our military guarantees to France were never disclosed by Asquith, the Prime Minister, and Grey, the Foreign Secretary, to their colleagues in the government. It would be hard to think of a more momentous secret, because it determined the participation of Britain in a war in which a million British lives were lost. Again, in the immediate post-war period, Clement Attlee, the Prime Minister, took the decision that Britain should make its own nuclear weapons in consultation with close political friends and advisers but without ever informing the full Cabinet, because he did not trust the wisdom or the discretion of some – indeed most – of his colleagues. That, again, was a momentous decision, the consequences of which are still with us. Whether or not it was prudent for a tiny section of the ruling elite to make these commitments itself and in total secrecy, it was certainly not democratic. And so critical were they, that it makes one wonder whether Britain can be called a working democracy in any sense which has meaning.

Let no one argue that central decisions of foreign and defence policy cannot be taken through the democratic process, directly or in spirit. That defeatist proposition would be unacceptable in the United States, where it runs counter to the US constitution, in letter and substance. It ought to be unacceptable here as well. To give one example: the decision of the British government in 1949 to initiate and sign the North Atlantic Treaty, which thereafter has remained the central fact in British foreign policy to this day, was a democratic one, in so far as we can judge these things. It was supported by all three parties and by an overwhelming majority of Members of Parliament. Every index of public opinion, such as the media and the opinion polls, endorsed the decision and continued to do so. The fact that a small political minority opposed it, and campaigned might and main to reverse it, and never over many years met with the slightest response from public opinion, is itself proof that the nation was happy with the policy. So foreign-policy-making and democracy can be reconciled.

That has not, alas, been the working assumption of successive British governments. It is certainly not the assumption on which the Foreign Office tenders its advice. Some great British statesmen, such as Lord Palmerston and Winston Churchill, have sought to make foreign policy in conjunction with the people, and they have been held in peculiar detestation by the Foreign Office mandarins. But most of our leaders have taken the view: 'Not in front of the children', and preserved the arcana. They do so to this day; indeed, perhaps more in this day than ever. Douglas Hurd, our Foreign Secretary at the time of writing, has a special 'not-in-front-of-the-children' tone of voice, and an even more revealing 'we-know-best' expression on his face. He would have agreed with Bismarck, who dismissed the claims of democracy with a brutal, 'Foreign affairs cannot be settled in the nursery.'

Yet the history of post-war Britain suggests that, in the long term, the instincts and understanding of the people are more likely to be right, in foreign affairs no less than in domestic ones, than the opinions of the 'experts'. In the late 1940s, the British political establishment, and the sub-section of it known as 'the foreign affairs community', while politely applauding the efforts of Jean Monnet and others to plan for a united Europe, indicated that a 'great power' like Britain, with global responsibilities, could not be expected to participate. We would be a 'benevolent observer' but our true interests lay elsewhere. This haughty and condescending tone was maintained into the early 1950s, when the first bricks of the European edifice were being laid down.

There was one important exception to this consensus of the elite. Winston Churchill, then as so often at odds with the establishment, was unhappy that our attitude to the European vision was so chilly. With his great love of France – in the crisis of the 1940s he had actually proposed a national union with the stricken Third Republic – and still more with his remarkable intuition and instinct for the future, he felt that Britain might be missing an important opportunity. He sensed, too, that the bulk of the people shared his hunch and felt that, if a great experiment in the future was beginning only 23 miles from our shores, we ought to be taking part in it. But he was an old man, with many other preoccupations, particularly the business of rebuilding the Atlantic Alliance and strengthening the free world's defences against an aggressive and increasingly formidable Soviet Russia. His close colleague Sir Anthony Eden and the Foreign Office were strongly opposed to any diversion of our efforts in a specifically European direction. They saw Britain's foreign commitments in terms of an elaborate and elegant global model, with London as the pivot of a series of concentric rings – the geographical ring of Europe, the constitutional ring of the British Commonwealth, and the defensive ring of the North Atlantic. Britain was the common factor in all these structures, and for that reason the kind of organic participation demanded of it in the new Europe was out of the question – it would conflict with its other roles, of which leadership of the Commonwealth was by far the most important.

Churchill was suspicious of this neat global diagram drawn up by the mandarins, feeling it had more to do with rosy aspirations than realities. He had led Britain during five years of total war, he knew how limited its resources were and how fragile was its grip on great power status. He had been all for the empire and keeping India. But with those gone, he was disinclined to put much faith in a paper arrangement termed 'the British Commonwealth'. Better to invest in a solid, historical entity like Europe, which was in any event nearer. The people shared these misgivings. They had loved the empire, cheered it, fought for it, worked for it. It was something they could grasp: red on the map, solid on the ground, ownership established in the freehold title deeds of perpetual Crown Colonies, linked together by ports and trading routes, protected by sea and air bases and by an all-weather, all-ocean Royal Navy. That was real. If they could not have it, so be it. But they could not be conned into thinking the Commonwealth was a substitute. It was vague, nebulous, intangible, impermanent, something built by diplomats on paper, not by pioneers and swordsmen on the spot. They looked at the Commonwealth and they smelt a rat. And how right they – and Churchill – were was proved a few years later in 1956, when Britain, embattled over Suez, found the Commonwealth a broken reed. Worse: Jawaharlal Nehru, leader of the Commonwealth's largest member state, led the United Nations pack against us!

However, at the time, the establishment had its way and Britain declined to take part. When the Coal–Steel Pool came into existence in August 1952, Britain was not a member. Nor would it have anything to do with the proposed European Defence Community, or 'European Army', though it pressed France to ratify the proposal; and when the French National Assembly rejected it, in summer 1954, the British Foreign Office had the gall to accuse the French government of being 'anti-European'. All the same, when negotiations opened for the expansion of the Coal–Steel Pool into the European

Common Market Britain did not apply to become a member. On 25 March 1957 the Treaty of Rome was signed without it. Instead, Britain created a lacklustre alternative of other non-participating European states, called the European Free Trade Area.

This was a fateful event in British, indeed in European, history. The absence of Britain in the negotiations meant that they took place not only without it, but to some extent against it. France, faced with the superior economic dynamism of Germany, already launched in its post-war 'miracle', was driven to a Faustian bargain. Under this, France reluctantly opened its markets to German manufactured goods but on condition that German money financed both the reduction of France's huge and inefficient peasant agricultural sector and also the creation of a new French industrial base. This bargain, known as the Common Agricultural Policy, became the financial and emotional heart of the Treaty of Rome and of the Brussels organisation it brought into being. It proved acceptable to Germany, and enormously valuable to France (and Italy), because it enabled France to reduce its peasant sector from over a third to less than a fifth and at the same time to industrialise south-east France. But it was fatal to the kind of Europe Jean Monnet had originally wished to bring into being. He envisaged the European economy being driven by market forces. The Common Agricultural Policy introduced the notion of subsidy – of so-called 'rich' areas subsidising so-called 'poor' areas. Once the principle of subsidy was introduced it spread and became the principal *raison d'être* of the Community. And, because subsidies involved the collection and transfer of large sums of money, a substantial bureaucracy had to be brought into existence to administer the process. Thus the Brussels we know came into lusty life: a huge machine of international officials, creating and circulating regulations which are then enforced by comparable pyramids of bureaucrats in the member states. It is inconceivable that this would have happened had Britain helped to write the original treaty.

The British people were not a consenting party to this huge missed opportunity. They were never consulted. 'Europe' played no part in the elections of 1950, 1951, 1954 and 1959.

There was no debate between the two great parties of the state, Labour and the Conservatives. The Labour leadership, like the Tory elite, was initially just as hostile to 'Europe', though for different reasons. It saw the Common Market not so much as an affront to British sovereignty and incompatible with the Commonwealth and the 'Special Relationship' with America, as a capitalist concern which, if Britain joined, would block Britain's own 'road to socialism'. Then, during the 1960s, faced with the continuing mediocre performance of the British economy and the rapid expansion of the six Common Market powers, there was an internal change of heart within both the Labour and the Conservative elites. On 10 August 1961 Harold Macmillan's Conservative government formally applied for British membership. On 14 January 1963, President de Gaulle angrily vetoed the application. On 14 May 1967 Harold Wilson's Labour government signalled a comparable change of view by reapplying for entry. Two days later, de Gaulle again imposed his veto. Not until de Gaulle himself had been pushed off the scene was the way to British membership open and only in June 1971, after a year of bitter negotiations, were the terms of British entry agreed.

Thus, thanks to the misjudgements and vacillations of Britain's ruling class, Britain missed the decade and a half when the new Europe was formulated, and the institution which came into being was in many respects alien to it. When the elites confessed their errors, Britain joined in the role of a tardy supplicant rather than a progenitor. There was nothing democratic about this late conversion either. Harold Wilson did not put forward European membership as a main plank in his 1964 election campaign – his change of mind was an afterthought, dating from 1966, and the electorate was not consulted about it. Nor was Europe an issue in the 1970 election, because by then all three parties had agreed on entry. Parliament approved the terms agreed by the Heath government by a Commons vote of 356–244, on 28 October 1971. But polls showed a majority of the British people were opposed to entry of what was now seen as an alien institution, and the previous month the Labour Party conference, for what that was worth, had voted against entry by a five-to-one majority. The

British people were not given a chance to express their views on the matter until June 1975, by which time membership was a *fait accompli* and the British economy had already been re-adjusted to the change. The referendum held then was not about joining the Common Market, but leaving it, and a frightened electorate, told by all three parties, the media, the leaders of British industry and the establishment *en masse* that such another change of course would be disastrous, opted for safety first and the status quo, by 67.2 per cent to 32.8. I took part in this campaign, and a very dispiriting and defeatist business it was, the fearfully acquiescent outnumbering the genuinely enthusiastic by about a hundred to one. It is worth noting the background to this vote: with the trade union barons running the economy, in so far as anyone was, during the previous month the pound sterling had lost 25.2 per cent of its value on the foreign exchanges, and inflation had reached a record 22 per cent.

Thus the British elite made a gigantic mess of Britain's participation in the great adventure of European unity. As a result the British people were obliged to join an organisation they had not created and did not find congenial. Nor did the story of disasters end there. In the 1980s, the Brussels Eurocrats and their allies among the elites holding power in the various European capitals pressed forward from the Common Market towards the idea of a European federal union. The first step was the European Exchange Rate Mechanism, forcing currencies of EC members into narrow bands of convergence; the next was the creation of a common currency and reserve bank, proposals for which were outlined in a treaty signed at Maastricht, which likewise laid down the final timetable for union.

Creating a federal union out of sovereign states is one of the greatest tests of human political ingenuity. Unless the process is carried out democratically, in spirit and not just in the letter, such a union is bound to end in tears, and probably in blood too. The calamitous disintegration of the USSR and the fiendish civil war in former Yugoslavia are examples of what ultimately happens when federations are imposed on reluctant nationalities. Post-war history is littered with the debris of failed federations created by due constitutional process: in the

West Indies, in the Middle East, in Central Africa, Malaysia and elsewhere.

The one outstanding model of a successful federal union is the United States. America's founding fathers contrived in the 1780s to bring together thirteen sovereign republics within a constitutional framework which has endured more than two hundred years. Thomas Jefferson, speaking for the founders, said he wanted a constitution which would endure: for that reason, amendments would be possible, but they would not be easy. In fact, the US constitution has been amended more than a score of times: but its essential framework, embodying its spirit, remains unaltered. There is no historical parallel for such longevity of a written constitution on this scale: during the same period, for instance, France has endured twelve enacted constitutions and five republics. How did the Americans succeed, where so many have failed?

There were two main reasons. First, the constitution itself was the product of a generation of cultured statesmen remarkable for their political literacy. It is written in clear and often beautiful English, which all can understand, and indeed easily memorise, as countless American schoolchildren have done. All constitutions require interpretation in the courts, but the US constitution has served as a sturdy and unbreakable plinth on which several generations of Supreme Court justices have erected a remarkable edifice of firm rulings. The American constitution is a testimony to the truth that, in politics, words are of supreme importance and require to be chosen with care and skill – indeed, in constitutional matters they require a touch of genius.

Second, the constitution was democratically presented and endorsed by the entire American people. Of course in the 1780s America was not yet a formal democracy; not even all adult white males had the vote, except in certain areas. But it was fast heading that way and, more important, it was already a democracy in spirit. The founding fathers were a self-conscious elite, who believed they were called to supply leadership and general guidance. But they accepted that all must be done with the people and nothing against the people. They showed a much greater ability to interpret and embody the general will than the French revolutionary leaders, supposedly devoted to Rousseau's principles, were to display in the next decade.

The way in which the US constitution was 'sold' remains a democratic model two centuries later. At the highest level it was explained by its authors and supporters in the *Federalist Papers*, which remains one of the great textbooks of political philosophy. It was promulgated in handbills and posters, printed in hundreds of newspapers great and small, commented upon, criticised, attacked and defended in thousands of newspaper and magazine articles and, most important of all, debated in every kind of assembly from the village tavern and town meeting to the state legislatures themselves. No nation in history has come into being amidst such intense, informed and prolonged discussion. And it was precisely because this first written constitution was made thoroughly familiar to ordinary people and won their approval, that it has survived, where so many others have failed ignominiously.

There are two other points to be borne in mind about the difficulties of creating federations. First, the Americans started out with huge advantages: they had a common language, written and spoken; a common literature; a common legal system and political culture; and for the most part a common religion. The thirteen states had never fought each other – quite the contrary: they had recently fought together as blood brothers in a victorious war for their independence. Nevertheless, despite these factors working in its favour, and despite the democratic manner of its endorsement, the constitution came under threat, in 1812 and after, from a separatist New England and in 1818 from a separatist South; the tensions were only resolved forty years later in an appalling civil war. The US federal constitution was finally cemented by the blood of a million fallen citizen-soldiers.

I emphasise the model of the US constitution precisely because it was totally ignored by the elite planning European federal union and seeking to impose it on the people. The work was done mainly by Francophones, and it is a lamentable fact that French schoolchildren are taught little or nothing of American history. It is regarded as a mere appendix of English history, itself of little importance in French state school curricula. Jean Monnet himself was an exception to this rule, for he not only knew a lot about Anglo-American history but was a student of the US constitution and realised its relevance. He grasped the spirit of American democracy, something which eludes a great many clever Continentals, who tend to regard Americans as only-recently civilised barbarians who have nothing to teach the Old World. So far as I can see, Jacques Delors, the principal architect of Maastricht and its adoption process, learned nothing whatever from Monnet, a man he once served, and paid no attention at all to the American precedent. He was irritated by the notion that Frenchmen could be taught anything. He found speaking and reading English difficult and felt under no obligation to start learning history again to please *les Anglo-Saxons*.

Yet there were pressing reasons why those who wanted a smooth transition to a federal Europe should have sought to take on board the American experience. They started out with many fewer advantages than the founding fathers. Europe has no common language and, despite the growing availability of English as an international tongue, is taking no steps to acquire one. Quite the contrary: the Brussels Francophones do everything in their power to have basic Eurotexts written in French alone, at least in the first instance. When Jacques Delors was asked by the Scandinavians why his press conferences were conducted solely in French and why he refused to permit simultaneous translation into English, he replied with asperity, '*Parce que le français est le langage de la diplomatie*,' adding under his breath, '*et de la civilisation*.' Yet language conflicts have in the past destroyed not only federations but unitary states and are always a threat to harmony: and if Delors doubted this he need look no further than Belgium itself, where the dispute for mastery between Flemish and Walloons is endemic and often violent. Nor is the lack of a common language the only or even the chief handicap. Europe, far from having a common religion, has a long history of religious conflict, which itself has produced profound cultural divergences. Some are directly relevant to the making of Europe, for the Protestant north has an altogether less tolerant attitude to corruption in the public domain than the more easy-going Catholic south. There are profound racial differences, too, between Nordics, Anglo-Saxons, Germans, Latins, Celts and Balkans. Perhaps most divisive of all, Europeans have spent the best part of two millennia fighting each other, their wars culminating in two global conflicts during this century which have left livid wounds not yet fully healed. The smoke of a thousand battlefields still drifts across the European landscape, and memories of countless injuries and outrages still linger in European hearts. Nothing is more calculated to resurrect ancient wrongs than an ill-drafted federal constitution which imposes new injustices.

Yet such considerations were ignored or disregarded by the men of Maastricht. The treaty itself must be the most ill-written and impenetrable in the whole of diplomatic history. Written jointly by bureaucrats and lawyers, it is a fiendish mixture of the jargon of both. Few have read it through. Fewer still have understood it. Its very size is baffling. Its 250 pages mean nothing in isolation because they amend 1100 pages of existing EC treaties which must be read in conjunction. The treaty was deliberately conceived as an anti-democratic document to be understood by an elitist group of lawyer-bureaucrats and then imposed on the people. The notion that it was ever intended to be 'sold' to ordinary citizens is inconceivable – quite the reverse: it was written in hieratic language precisely to ensure the continuing rule of the elect Brussels priesthood.

The way in which Maastricht was ratified was a cynical mockery of the democratic process. In every one of the twelve states, the governments which signed the treaty had built-in majorities in parliaments where all the principal parties supported union. There was thus no possibility of the issue being put to voters in general elections. Nor, in most cases, was there much chance of serious debate in national parliaments, before the rubber-stamping began. Three countries held referenda. In the Republic of Ireland the result was wholly predictable because the Common Agricultural Policy and other subsidy provisions of the Treaty of Rome meant that Dublin got five dollars from Brussels for every one contributed, and under Maastricht stood to gain at least $5 billion more: the Irish had been bought and paid for. But the Irish and the Greeks, who also gain in the proportion of five to one, were the only enthusiasts. When France, almost as an afterthought, held a referendum on Maastricht, the Mitterrand régime won only by a whisker, and would indeed have lost had not the entire French business and media establishment, led of course by the state television and radio networks, campaigned for a Yes vote throughout. In Denmark, the political elites, though similarly backed by business and the media, actually contrived to lose, albeit by a narrow margin. This should have ended the treaty, for one of its few clear provisions laid down that unless Maastricht were ratified by all twelve powers it was null, and the Danish constitution provides that more than one referendum cannot be taken on the same issue.

What followed this No vote convinced me that the Euro-fanatics do not care a damn for the rule of law and will cheerfully violate any treaty, in the letter and in the spirit, if they think they can get away with it. The first reaction in Brussels to the Danish No was that the Danes must be punished by being put into a 'slow lane' while the 'fast track' eleven went forward – something not provided for by Maastricht at all. On second thoughts, it was decided to hold a second referendum after the Danish government went through a pantomime of 'amending' the treaty. The Danish establishment, and other European business interests, spent vast sums in ensuring a Yes vote the second time, and every single Danish newspaper, with one marginal exception, bullied the poor Danes into line. I took part in this second campaign and I am proud to say that my public meeting in Copenhagen attracted more Danes than a similar meeting the day before addressed by their Prime Minister (notorious, to be sure, as the dullest speaker recorded in the history of European narcolepsy). The result was a foregone conclusion: but the Danes, as many assured me, voted from fear, not from any belief in European federal union.

That left Britain. As the cradle of democracy, Britain should have given its European partners an elementary lesson in how the people should be consulted. Many of the other eleven states had only recently acquired the right to vote fully and freely, having endured all kinds of absolute monarchies and dictator-ships: for them to submit to yet another pseudo-utopian frame of government was nothing new. But for Britain, with a thousand years of parliamentary sovereignty behind it, it was a different matter. The British were being asked to renounce their independent government and, on behalf of not just themselves but their progeny, to embrace rule by a treaty written in incomprehensible legal-bureaucratic gobbledygook. This, surely, required a special effort to consult the people and abide by their wishes.

No such thing. I think it is fair to say that the John Major government, and the bureaucratic and business interests associated with it, from the Foreign Office to the Confederation of British Industry, were absolutely determined from the start to get Maastricht ratified whatever the British people felt about it, and more particularly if the people should demonstrate their hostility. Everything was to be done 'for their own good', the maxim of dictators through the ages. Every effort was made to reduce debate to the narrowest possible limits. A referendum was refused, repeatedly, as 'quite unconstitutional' – ignoring the fact that Maastricht itself in effect abolished the British constitution, for ever. Steps were even taken to conceal the text of the treaty and deliberately to twist its meaning. Ministers were instructed never to use the word 'federal' in their speeches (a veto later extended, in 1994, to all Conservatives, by Tory Central Office), though the treaty is manifestly, from start to finish, a federalist instrument. There were long delays in even producing an official English version of the text, and when finally available it was put on sale only in limited numbers and at an outrageously high price. On this point we were shamefully taught a lesson in democracy by both the Danes and the French, who distributed millions of copies of the text free.

The determination of the Major government to push Maastricht through Parliament at any cost became all the more extraordinary when ministers themselves began privately to lose all faith in the practicability of its central provisions. Obviously, federal union could not begin to work without a common currency. The Exchange Rate Mechanism prepared the way for this by forcing individual governments and central banks to maintain predetermined fixed exchange rates, within narrow bands, by ferocious use of high interest rates. So long as

Margaret Thatcher was Prime Minister there was no chance of Britain joining a federal Europe against the will of the people. She had battled fiercely to reopen the poor financial deal her predecessor Edward Heath had secured, and thus saved British taxpayers hundreds of millions of pounds in contributions to the Brussels coffers. She had also opposed British membership of the ERM, believing this device was fundamentally unworkable and, in any event, deprived Britain of the right to its own interest-rate policy in pursuit of its national needs. But in 1988 she had bowed to the will of most of her colleagues, and much establishment financial opinion, and allowed Britain to enter the ERM, though in a wide not a narrow band. This proved to be a disastrous error, and she later bitterly blamed herself for allowing others to overcome her reason and instincts. Belonging to the ERM tied Britain to Germany's interest-rate policy, kept artificially high on account of the unexpectedly large inflationary effect of German reunification. As a result the British recession, which began in 1989, was not only deepened but prolonged into the most persistent since the 1930s. Incalculable damage was inflicted on the British economy, and grievous sufferings were meted out to the British people, many of whom lost their jobs and houses as a direct result of high interest rates.

When Margaret Thatcher was hustled into retirement in 1990 and withdrew her strong grip on the country, the economic consequences of ERM membership became more severe and obvious. In October 1992, John Major and his Chancellor of the Exchequer, Norman Lamont, having earlier sworn many oaths that in no circumstances would they leave the ERM, did precisely that, in shame and confusion. Britain's departure, followed by that of Italy, weakened the whole structure, which the following August virtually collapsed when France in its turn was forced by speculators to leave its narrow band. If the ERM did not work, how could Europe move forwards towards a common currency, of which that mechanism was the essential precursor? Doubts on this point were strengthened by the realisation that the German Bundesbank, the strongest financial institution in Europe, had deliberately undermined the parity first of Britain, then of

France, within the mechanism because its directors had no desire to see a common currency come into being. But if the ERM could not be made to work, and a common currency was thus ruled out in the foreseeable future, how could Maastricht bring into existence a federal Europe? The whole operation was beginning to look like a confidence trick, which the Eurocrats and their backers in the capitals of the twelve states could not abandon without fatal loss of face.

That is why Major and his colleagues – or some of them; others were less keen – decided to drum Maastricht through Parliament despite the fact that they believed it unworkable. So began in 1993 one of the most shameful episodes in the history of the House of Commons. The Maastricht Treaty had not been an issue at the 1992 election, so the government had no natural mandate to push it through. Moreover, opinion polls showed that a majority of voters, varying from narrow to overwhelming, disliked the treaty and still more its implications for Britain's future. The moral case, therefore, for a referendum on this specific issue was clear, and the polls indeed showed that between two-thirds and three-quarters of the British electorate wanted one. The anti-Maastricht MPs, mainly within the Conservative Party, felt therefore that they had a right to use every procedural means to overthrow the Commons majority in favour of the treaty which they argued was unrepresentative, at least to secure a referendum. On 22 July the government was actually defeated, by a combination of Tory rebels and opposition votes. The following day the government asked for a vote of confidence, which was naturally provided, since it had a normal working majority in the House of nineteen. But the vote of 22 July was never, strictly speaking, reversed. Although the treaty passed its third reading in the Commons, the government was never able to persuade a majority of MPs to support its own interpretation of what the treaty meant, and so fulfil the terms of ratification. There was, therefore, a bit of sleight-of-hand about the ratification itself, whose legality remains doubtful. Moreover, some of the votes were secured under duress. To reduce the number of rebels, government whips employed a combination of methods never before experienced in the lifetime of the most senior MPs. These included frog-marching an MP through the government lobby. Now, the use of physical 'persuasion' during a division was by no means unprecedented. In the 1580s, Sir Walter Raleigh, a bold and tactless man, was once howled down by the Commons for admitting shamelessly that he had often 'plucked at a man's sleeve' to prevent him voting. But Sir Walter acted as a private member. For the whips to use force, it might be argued, invalidated any vote so obtained. Moreover, force was not their only weapon. Their tactics included stirring up trouble in the constituencies of Tory MPs who threatened to vote against the government, and even telephoning their wives to point out that their husbands were jeopardising their careers and livelihoods by following their consciences. Whips also threatened to divulge details of unsavoury episodes in the lives of rebel MPs unless they toed the line. Conversely, honours, including knighthoods, were promised to MPs who resolved their doubts in the government's favour, and financial inducements were dangled in front of the constituencies of wavering Members. All in all, one would have to go back to the eighteenth century to find an example of a statute carried through the Commons by more corrupt and reprehensible means. In short, it is not clear whether even the law was complied with in forcing Maastricht through the Commons. It is quite certain that the vote carried no moral authority. The so-called ratification by Britain of the Maastricht Treaty was both undemocratic and contrary to the principles of natural justice. Hence, as the grip of the Brussels bureaucracy on our country tightens, as the British discover that fewer and fewer matters can be settled in London, and that power over the minutest details of their lives is held increasingly across the Channel, deep in the recesses of continental Europe, by people who do not speak English and who have little in common with the British temperament, the way in which Maastricht was passed into British law will be remembered with growing bitterness and fury. The British people have shown in the past, repeatedly, that they know how to bring lawless governments to book, and for many of us the story of Maastricht is not yet finished.

The passage of the treaty through the House was such a sordid story as to raise doubts about other aspects of modern

British parliamentary life. And once these doubts are examined
they raise fresh ones, until scepticism spreads about the whole
nature of our parliamentary system, and how far it conforms to
the most elementary conditions of democracy. Is Parliament,
indeed, an undemocratic sham?

CHAPTER FIVE

A Society Fit for Criminals to Live In

Let us be clear about what can fairly be expected from a parliamentary democracy, and what cannot. Neither Parliament nor the government is under moral compulsion to do exactly what a majority of the electorate wants, on any particular issue, at any particular time. 'Instant democracy' cannot be made to work in a parliamentary system, and would be a pretty ignoble thing if it could. Members of Parliament should be honourable and dignified men and women, intelligent, experienced, knowledgeable and independent-minded, exercising wide powers of discretion as to timing, opportunity, manner and degree in carrying out the popular will. What is required of them, however, in order for democracy to function and to be seen to function, is that over a period their decisions must broadly reflect public wishes on all matters of central importance in the life of the nation. If MPs cannot bend their wills and judgements to this extent, then they have no business serving in a parliamentary democracy. They should take up another trade, where they have no representative function, and where their egos are subjected only to the restraints of the market.

Parliament, then, must ultimately carry out the public's wishes. And there are two areas of policy on which this rule applies with particular force. The first is public finance. What does the government need to do to serve the public welfare adequately? What will this cost? And how should the money be raised? These fundamental questions go right to the heart of representative government. It was to answer them that knights of the shires and burgesses from the towns were first sent by the people to confer together in Parliament, in the thirteenth and fourteenth centuries. That is still their primary function today and nothing illustrates better the need for close accord, over a period, between MPs and electors. I shall come to this issue in the next chapter.

There is a second area of policy of almost equal importance: public order. Some would argue that, in the minds of most people, it is today of even more concern than taxation. That may well be so. But we can all agree that taxes and order are the two things uppermost in the minds of the public when they think of government and its impact on their lives. We all have to pay taxes in one way or another. And we are all affected, in our daily existence, by the degree of order which authority maintains in our society. Maintaining order was not the original function of Parliament. That was the king's job, for which he was provided with a prerogative. He was the original Leviathan, as Thomas Hobbes says, 'to keep them all in awe' and to prevent 'the life of man' from becoming 'solitary, poor, nasty, brutish and short'. The king was not elected; but if he failed in his role of Leviathan, he was removable, as King Stephen and King John, Edward II and Henry VI found to their cost. In time this Leviathan function was taken over by representative government, local and central, and in the first instance by Parliament, which determines the statutory framework within which order is maintained. Parliament is never more obliged to be responsive to and representative of the public will than when it is deciding how order can best be kept.

It is here that the parliamentary system has broken down almost completely in the last generation. For more than thirty years – some would say longer – Parliament and people have drifted further and further apart on this issue. As MPs have become more and more liberal, increasingly inclined to listen to fashionable theories of penology and act upon them, the people have remained obstinately and vehemently conservative, rejecting such theories with disbelief and anger. This fissure at the heart of our parliamentary system of government is bad enough in itself. But it has been rendered increasingly dangerous by the speed and inexorability with which crime has increased. In the 1930s it was easy and common for a man or woman to pass an entire lifetime in Britain without becoming a victim of crime, even of a petty kind. In the 1990s it would be inconceivable. Most people are victims of crime on average once a year; in many areas it is once a month, even once a week; and every single one of us is conscious of our vulnerability all the time. Thus crime, and its prevention and punishment, are matters of everyday importance to us all, and it is precisely against this background that Parliament and people have diverged. The people, perceiving this, have drawn their own conclusions. Ignoring the variety of conflicting explanations provided by 'experts', they are quite convinced that crime has risen to horrific and unacceptable levels precisely because their wishes have been ignored by successive governments which have adopted liberal policies in the teeth of popular dis-approval. They know that democracy has failed and that they are bearing the dire consequences of its failure. The result is not just cynicism, but rising anger.

Take, to begin with, the simple and central issue of murder. There are certain types of crime, financial fraud for instance, about which ordinary people are ignorant and know they are ignorant, and so have sensible reservations about how they should be treated. But the taking of human life is a matter on which everyone has views and is entitled to have views. It is the most basic of all issues of morality and has been a matter of natural and passionate concern to us all ever since Cain slew Abel. We may differ in our views about how murder should be regarded and dealt with, but all these views have equal moral worth. In murder, there is no moral expertise. The opinion of an illiterate labourer is as valid as that of the wisest judge. Each has only one life to lose. Each is liable to lose it in a murderous society; indeed the labourer's life, being less well protected, is more at risk. It would be fair to say that, in a society such as ours, where crime, especially violent crime, is increasing rapidly, the opinions of common men and women ought to carry even more weight than in a law-abiding society, precisely because the shadow of murder falls more threateningly over their lives.

Yet it is on this issue of murder that successive parliaments have shown themselves most contemptuous of public opinion. And this in itself is strange. In all my historical studies of different societies, from deep antiquity to the present, I have never come across one where the generality of people have expressed qualms about capital punishment. There seems to be a deep-rooted human instinct, expressed in all ages and races, that there are certain circumstances in which it is right for society to take the life of a culprit. The notion that life is sacred in all circumstances has always been a minority view, usually the view of a tiny minority.

Of course public opinion has varied enormously on how many should be capitally punished and for what crimes. If we take Britain, for instance, there is abundant evidence that ordinary people have never favoured executions on a large scale, particularly for crimes against property, however serious. In the late seventeenth and eighteenth centuries the decline of public belief in Hell undermined fear of eternal punishment as a deterrent. It produced, or was thought to have produced, a huge increase in crimes against property. Parliament responded in the most savage fashion, replacing fear of Hell with the fear of the rope. There is no evidence that it had any kind of popular mandate to do so. Quite the contrary. The most formidable of these eighteenth-century measures, the Waltham Black Act of 1723, which created fifty distinct capital offences for seven different groups of offenders, was aimed chiefly at deer-stealing and was passed at the behest of a small number of landowners and the custodians of royal parks. It was very unpopular and was largely unenforced for this reason. Juries would not convict or mobs would overturn the scaffold before offenders could be executed. Men, women and children could in theory be hanged in the eighteenth and nineteenth centuries for all kinds of crimes. Parliament said so. But in practice it was public opinion which determined who died. The notion that children (i.e. those under fourteen) were hanged for petty offences is a myth. We do not know how many, if any, children were hanged in the eighteenth century but there is only one documented execution of a child in the nineteenth century: John Bell, a thirteen-year-old, was hanged at Maidstone in 1831, for a pecularly atrocious murder. Under the pressure of public opinion, the number of those actually executed fell sharply at the end of the eighteenth century and the beginning of the nineteenth. MPs might not repeal the Black Code but ordinary people ensured it was increasingly null. In the 1790s only one in three of those capitally convicted died; by 1810 it had fallen to one in seveñ and by the mid-1830s to one in fourteen. The repeal of most of the capital statutes followed as a matter of course, though it took time, Parliament lagging well behind public opinion.

However, while public opinion in the nineteenth century gradually persuaded Parliament to limit capital punishment in effect to the crime of murder, its clemency stopped abruptly at this point. All the nineteenth- and early twentieth-century evidence confirms that most people were unwavering in their view that execution was, as a rule, the right punishment for murder. This is confirmed by modern opinion polls which show that between 70 and 85 per cent of the population favour capital punishment for most murders. It is useful to reflect why this should be so. All inquiries suggest that the public desire to punish capitally a convicted murderer is not based on a disregard for the value of human life. It is precisely because the public values human life above all things that it regards the unlawful taking away of it with such abhorrence and detestation; it is so shocked by the *fact* of murder that it demands this unique crime be paid for by a unique punishment. The taking of a human life by the state is an awesome event, a lawful killing which, by its very horror and solemnity, draws attention to the unique wickedness of murder. The state does this appalling thing to bring home to everyone, men, women and children, that to steal another's life is the greatest of crimes. An execution is a spectacularly effective way of demonstrating society's outrage and, in theory at least, it ought to be carried out in public, as in most societies it was until quite modern times. Lord Palmerston always argued that publicity was an essential part of the salutary effect of capitally punishing a murderer, and that in any case it could not be right for the state to kill

anyone in secrecy. Be that as it may, the public agreed with
Palmerston's conclusions: they thought it right that a hanging
should be carried out in the open, where all could see, and
ponder. That was part of the catharsis, whereby society as a
whole atoned to God for the fact that one of His creatures had
been wantonly destroyed. We think of public executions in
terms of city mobs and drunken disorder. But most executions
were carried out in the countryside, before solemn little
gatherings of neighbours, often on their knees and awed by the
event in which they felt themselves to be necessary participants.
Wilful murder was rare among them and a public hanging
helped to exorcise it. They marked the occasion by changing
the names of local landmarks. In the Quantock Hills, where I
have a house, there are innumerable place names which testify
to the unique power of murder to burn itself into the popular
memory: Dead Woman's Ditch, Walton's Gibbet, Jake's Neck,
and so forth. However, it was the big city executions and the
unseemly events which surrounded them which caught the eye
and offended the sensibilities of the intelligentsia and the
chattering classes of mid-nineteenth-century London. A
vociferous campaign was mounted to have hanging carried out
within the secrecy of the prison and before the fewest possible
witnesses, and in 1868 they had their way. Seven years earlier,
in 1861, Parliament had in effect limited capital punishment to
murder, and it did so with the full approbation of the public. It
was in 1868 that the divergence began.

Not until the 1960s, however, did it widen into an unbridgeable chasm. The fact that the opponents of capital
punishment, despite their well-financed and well-organised
lobbies and their dominance of the upper reaches of publishing
and the media, took an entire century to carry out the rest of
their programme testifies to the obstinacy of the ordinary
people and the reluctance of many MPs to ignore their views.
However, the abolitionists finally succeeded during that
memorable decade in which all the familiar landmarks of
society were moved or scrapped. From 1963 hangings ceased in
Britain, and from 1965 they became, not in theory but for all
practical purposes, unlawful.
7 I felt at the time, though I publicly supported the measure,

uneasy in my mind. For one thing, I knew many of those who were most prominent in campaigning for abolition – Sidney Silverman, Victor Gollancz, Gerald Gardiner and so on – and found them to be almost without exception strange and highly emotional people: not at all the kind I would go to for prudent advice on anything important. They claimed to speak with the voice of reason, and they produced masses of statistics and all kinds of other 'objective' evidence to prove their cucumber-cool rationality. But it was plain to me that their approach to the subject was not a matter of proof, but of faith. They believed in abolition in the way that most of us believe in God. Abolition was an important item in a secular creed which had replaced Christianity or Judaism in their lives. Their minds had never been open on the subject, and at no point had they weighed the evidence, especially on the key issue of whether capital punishment deterred certain kinds of murderer, with a view to making up their minds. Their minds were more firmly closed to doubt than any prison door. I have never in my life met any kind of enthusiast less open to persuasion than an abolitionist of capital punishment. They look for 'evidence' – and if necessary manufacture it: Gollancz, in particular, was quite capable of faking figures – solely to justify conclusions which had already been immovably reached.

I agreed with the decision to abolish capital punishment at the time, as I think did many others, for two reasons. First, I thought it possible that the abolitionists might be right in arguing that ending hanging would not be followed by an appreciable increase in murder. Second, I believed that the repeated assurances given in Parliament, that when the rope was replaced by mandatory life imprisonment the sentence really would mean 'life', might just conceivably be genuine. In short, I decided to judge this fundamental change in our criminal code, for which there was no popular mandate, by results.

What has happened since the mid-1960s has, of course, justified the worst fears of those who opposed any change at all. In the last thirty years, the number of homicides has increased dramatically. The full extent of the increase has been disguised by the policy of classifying many killings, which until the 1960s would have been labelled plain murder, as manslaughter, and by a prodigious extension of the notion of 'diminished responsibility'. The authorities, once committed to the policy of abolition, have tried to keep the murder rate down by changing the definition of crimes and massaging the statistics. Even so, the number of unequivocal murders has multiplied. They have also increased in savagery. Indiscriminate mass killings by the IRA and other terrorist groups, the slaughter of very old people and of tiny children, the use of torture in killing, the levity and even pointlessness with which human lives are now taken – all these forms of atrocity have markedly increased, and the rate of increase grows all the time.

However, though the numbers and ferocity of killings have risen sharply, the way in which the convicted killers are punished has been progressively diluted. There is now no longer the smallest pretence that life imprisonment means what it says. The abolition of capital punishment has coincided with the adoption by the authorities of a *de facto* policy that criminals of all kinds should be imprisoned for the shortest time compatible with elementary public safety: in other words, that the policy of using prison simply as punishment should be abandoned. This change of policy in the use of prison was not determined democratically. It was not submitted to the voters in an election by any of the three parties. It figured in no manifesto or party programme. No MP seeking re-election told the voters this was what he proposed to support. It was not mentioned in any Queen's Speech. Parliament did not embody it in any statute. It simply, and stealthily, became part of administrative and judicial practice. Of course we were all uncomfortably aware that it was happening, since we noticed prison sentences were getting shorter and shorter, and the length of time criminals actually served in prison was, on average, only half of their nominal sentence. But the first indication that the shortest possible sentences were *official* policy was given in a series of interviews with senior judges carried out by the *Observer* in autumn 1993.

It is not even clear why this new policy was adopted. One reason appears to be the failure of the authorities to build enough prisons. Another appears to be the simple fact that, because of the increase in crime, such prisons as exist are full. A third is that, because of the internationally-enforced 'rights' enjoyed by convicts, the cost of keeping a prisoner has risen sharply, to between £20,000 and £50,000 a year. In addition to these practical reasons, there appears to be, among those concerned with crime and punishment – judges, prison 'experts', probation officers, academic penologists – an increasing ideological reluctance to send anyone to prison at all. Long prison sentences are now regarded by the cognoscenti as 'bad policy', 'a confession of failure', 'inhuman', etc. As a result, those convicted of killing (in which I include manslaughter and criminals adjudged to be of diminished responsibility at the time of the crime) usually serve what would once have been regarded as short sentences. It is not uncommon nowadays for a convicted killer, especially if female, to walk from the court free. This is especially true of women who kill their husbands (though men are also benefiting from this leniency). The defence urges that the dead man was a monster of cruelty. The prosecutor does not consider it part of his/her duty to offer evidence to the contrary (the notion that the Crown represents the interests of the slain has become a dead letter). The jury convicts the accused, the evidence of the killing being incontrovertible. But the judge, in passing sentence, commiserates with the killer, points out that she has already been in custody a number of months while awaiting trial, and puts her on probation or gives her a suspended sentence. Now it may well be that, on such occasions, justice is done. But this kind of procedure was definitely not what Parliament, let alone an anxious public, had in mind when capital punishment was abolished in the mid-1960s. It is exactly the opposite of what Parliament had in mind. And such procedures certainly give the public the impression that, in the eyes of the law, killing another human being is not necessarily a serious offence these days.

Even those convicted of murder serve, on average, only thirteen years and two months. Life imprisonment has ceased to be the punishment for murder. In certain cases – such as the Moors Murderers and the Kray Twins – where the killings were peculiarly grievous, the authorities have not dared to release the criminals for fear of a public outcry and possible acts of revenge by the families of the victims. In certain other cases, the sentencing judge lays down a minimum term of years which the murderer must serve. These 'extra' years served affect the average. Hence most 'ordinary' murderers actually serve less than thirteen years in prison, some considerably less. The release of killers from prison after four, five or six years – or even after one or two –does not attract headlines. But it is known in the communities where they, and the victims, live. And this too adds to the public impression that authority no longer treats killing with particular seriousness. It is just a crime, like many others. Thus human life has lost the peculiar sanctity the law once accorded it. There is here a poignant irony. Victor Gollancz and his friends campaigned thirty years ago to end capital punishment because, as they said, of their reverence for human life. Their success has ended by devaluing it.

One result of murderers serving short sentences is that they live to kill again, in increasing numbers. At the time of the abolition of capital punishment this was discounted as a practical possibility, and those who warned about it were laughed at. What – eighty-year-old former murderers, released in their dotage, killing again? The possibility of murderers serving life killing inside prisons was, of course, considered. The abolitionists argued that this was a risk society simply had to take. Certainly, it is a risk that prison warders have to take, and some have indeed paid with their lives. So have many prisoners. Since a violent convicted murderer, serving many years in prison because of the peculiar atrocity of his crimes, cannot be punished further, it is all one to him whether he kills again or not – and the prospect of being murdered by a fellow inmate within a confined space has been added to the terrors of incarceration. But what comes as a real surprise to many people – and would have astounded those MPs who voted for abolition in 1963 – is the growing number of innocent members of the public who are now killed by convicted murderers set free to roam the world. Between 1963 and 1989, no fewer than fifty-nine people were killed by those released after serving sentences for murder or manslaughter. Since 1989 the kill-again rate has doubled, from an average of two a year to four, and a further thirteen people have died at the hands of recidivist killers. All seventy-two of these innocents might have lived their natural span if hanging had been retained, or even if those who abolished it had kept their promises about 'life imprisonment'. That is a sombre fact for the abolitionists to have aboard their consciences.

While we are considering the growing number of unlawful killings which occur in Britain – many of them as a direct result of the abolition of capital punishment – it is convenient to consider the cases of murders which take place because of the failure of authority to imprison those with manifest homicidal tendencies. This too is a growing category, and nothing angers the public more. A typical case came to light in January 1994, when a paedophile called Colin Hatch was convicted of strangling a seven-year-old boy. This man had a long record, it emerged, of offences against small children, some of them violent. Two years before, he had carried out a vicious attack upon a boy of eight. A psychiatrist recommended that he be sent to a secure mental hospital, Broadmoor. But Broadmoor declined to accept him as he was 'not dangerous enough'. He was sent instead to a young offenders institution, from which he dispatched a series of letters 'looking forward' to his release. One letter, which was seen of course by the authorities, read: 'All young boys and girls aged between eight and eleven had better be ready.' The parents of the child he subsequently murdered were naturally bitter about the callous failure of authority to prevent their son being strangled. The judge, sentencing the man to life imprisonment, added, 'It is not possible to envisage circumstances in which you could be safely released from prison.' No doubt the man will indeed serve many years in gaol. But he is only twenty-one, and in the light of recent experience, one wonders how soon he will in fact be free, possibly to kill children again.

The increasingly relaxed attitude of the authorities towards killing arouses more public anger than any other aspect of criminal justice. It is the biggest single factor in the chasm which now separates Parliament and the general public. The abolition of capital punishment for murder is not the only point on which rulers and people differ. The determination of the authorities to keep as many convicted criminals, and especially 'young offenders', as possible out of prison constantly angers the public. The expression 'young offenders' gives the impression that the crimes perpetrated by this category are, somehow, of a minor variety. In fact youth increasingly leads the field in wickedness, not just in quantity but in barbarity. Not only are more than half of all offences in Britain committed by those under twenty-one; but youths, and sometimes children, are responsible for a growing number of crimes so odious as to be almost beyond human comprehension.

For instance, the 1980s and 1990s have seen a savage increase in burglaries on the premises of very old women, many of whom have also been raped. The Home Office does not compile figures of crimes which come into this category, which was virtually unknown a generation ago, and analysis is dependent on fragmentary newspaper reports which of course are not inclusive. Some of these crimes are the work of habitual offenders: for instance, in February 1992 a man was gaoled for sexually assaulting and severely beating an eighty-eight-year-old woman. He had already served an eight-year (i.e. four-year) sentence for raping a fifty-year-old woman, and the friends of the eighty-eight-year-old lady, who was lucky to survive at all, angrily demanded how he came to be at liberty to commit this outrage. However, many of these rapes of the elderly are the work of young, sometimes very young, men, searching for quite small sums of money in the homes of pensioners, and adding sexual gratification as a bonus. Women of eighty-four, seventy-one and eighty-three were robbed, raped, trussed up and placed in their own wardrobes to prevent them giving the alarm during 1993; the only criminal apprehended was a seventeen-year-old. In June 1992 a sixteen-year-old was convicted at Norwich of raping a woman of one hundred. In another terrifying case in 1992 an eighty-eight-year-old was left with a fractured skull after being raped by two youths and forced to carry out what were described as 'perverted sexual acts'.

At the other end of the age scale, more and more serious crimes against children are being committed by youths or even by children themselves. The murder of four-year-old James

Bulger by two eleven-year-olds attracted headlines in 1993, but this fortunately is regarded by police as untypical, as yet; far more common are serious sexual and other assaults. More horrific still are cases of juveniles who steal cars and carry out ram-raids, setting fire to shops and other buildings and driving at reckless speeds through residential districts. Such crimes produced a score of deaths of innocent passers-by in 1993. Recent statutes make it extremely difficult to convict juveniles of offences or to impose sentences which the public regard as appropriate. Youngsters who kill pedestrians while driving stolen cars often walk out of court free or are sent for institutional 'treatment' which the public does not regard as punitive. Police frankly confess that many child offenders, and even youths, are never brought to court at all as they cannot be bothered to go through all the paperwork involved, knowing that the punishment, even if a conviction is secured, will be derisory. Great anger was caused in 1993 when a fifteen-year-old who had been convicted of a long list of crimes, some of them serious, was sent on an eight-week safari in Africa costing £7000 as part of his 'cure', was released on his return and promptly stole another car. Local council-tax payers had to finance this expensive comedy. Millions of honest working-class families, whose tax burden is now considerable, burn with rage when they read in their newspapers of young criminals who, instead of being punished, are sent on sailing and adventure courses which are beyond the means of the average household. The public is still more incensed to discover that, under legislation passed against their wishes, some of the most prolific and destructive criminals cannot be punished at all. A case came to light in February 1994 of a criminal boy who, between the ages of twelve and fourteen, broke into 879 shops and businesses in the Carshalton area, burgled 113 homes and robbed four banks; he also stole eighty-seven cars. The value of the goods he stole was over £2 million. It took the police six days just to list the crimes he admitted. The boy had been arrested forty times. But though old enough to be a successful, large-scale habitual criminal, the law said he was not old enough to be held in custody, still less in prison. The most the courts could sentence him to was a twelve-month supervision order. The law even forbade newspapers from publishing his name, though he is known to the angry community he has pillaged as Kid Crook.

There is a widespread feeling that, over the whole spectrum of crime and its punishment, Parliament and government ministers possess an entirely different set of standards and convictions from the people who elect them. The chasm between rulers and ruled is probably wider over crime than over any other issue. The fault lies in the way legislation is enacted. Parliament, as originally conceived in the later Middle Ages, existed not merely to raise taxes but, in return, to petition for redress of grievances. Often knights and burgesses would arrive already armed with drafts of statutes prepared by their constituents; these were then composed into formal bills and enacted. That, in its primitive way, was democracy. If that process were translated into modern terms, it would mean that MPs, come election-time, listened to the voices of their constituents, and arrived at the new parliament with a shopping-list of things their voters wanted done. The House of Commons would then deal with the most common complaints by passing laws to remedy them. That, again, would be democracy. But it does not happen. Elections are conducted by presenting voters with party programmes, drawn up at party headquarters often without much regard to what the public is supposed to want. Voters are never given the texts, or gists, of future statutes. Indeed, what happens in any one parliament often bears little relation to the manifesto of the victorious party.

Most key statutes nowadays are the work of specific groups of people: lobbyists for particular pressure groups, the senior civil servants with whom they deal in the relevant department, parliamentary draughtsmen and other lawyers. There is a ministerial input too, especially if the minister has strong views, is experienced and streetwise. But some ministers are non-entities and play virtually no part in legislation other than to push it through Parliament. Whitehall and Westminster now abound in what are known as 'communities'. There is the foreign affairs community, the social services community, the education community and so on. The crime-and-punishment community consists of the lobbyists from, for instance, the

Howard League for Penal Reform, the Prison Officers Association, the Association of Probation Officers, etc; civil servants who deal with these matters; academics in the related 'disciplines'; and specialist media correspondents – plus MPs who happen to be interested in the topic and who are often themselves lobbyists, paid or unpaid. These small, incestuous groups, all of whom know each other and meet constantly at conferences, teach-ins, overseas junkets and the like, tend to be overwhelmingly liberal in outlook, or at least attached to fashionable new theories. The existence of this 'community' explains how the notorious Criminal Justice Act (1991) got onto the statute book. This Act did a large number of things to hamper law enforcement. One of them was to make it difficult, if not impossible, for courts to take previous offences into account when sentencing. To the despair of the police, it obliged courts to treat habitual offenders as first-time offenders. The minister most responsible for the Act was Douglas Hurd, Home Secretary during its gestation period. He is a celebrated elitist, who has a marked preference for working with Whitehall/Westminster 'communities' (not for nothing is he a political pupil of Edward Heath) and what he would regard as a healthy contempt for the opinion of ordinary people. This Act, important though it was to the public, did not figure except *en passant* in the 1987 election manifesto, was never subject to public debate and was comparatively little discussed in Parliament. When it finally came into effect it aroused an immediate uproar among the public and provoked the resignation, in disgust, of numerous long-serving magistrates. As a result, the then Home Secretary, Kenneth Clarke, who had no particular attachment to his predecessor's baby, declined to get into an argument but simply suspended one or two of its more offensive provisions, preparatory to correcting them in the 1993 Criminal Justice Act. This was an act of belated if limited democracy, though carried out in a breathless and therefore defective manner. It provoked cries of fury from the lobbyists who had produced the measure, and their letters of protest, published in *The Times*, can be read by anyone anxious to identify the organisations responsible for the disastrous 1991 Act.

Against this legislative background, it is no surprise that crime has increased, is increasing and is quite certain to increase still further to the turn of the century and beyond. Of course there are other reasons for the growth of crime besides laws which obstruct the enforcement process. But this kind of legislation is of particular consequence both because it is undemocratic, destroying public belief in our system of government – and public confidence in the system is itself an important element in law enforcement – and also because it has a shattering effect on police morale. The work of the police in our society is, in any event, becoming progressively more difficult. They are overwhelmed by the sheer volume of crime of all kinds. Since the 1960s, in addition to the rapid rise in traditional crimes, they have had to deal with new categories, such as computer crime and entirely new types of financial and commercial crime, which consume police time in prodigious quantities. To top it all, they now have to devote a large part of their resources to combating terrorism, not merely in following up bomb outrages and bringing those responsible to justice but in carrying out whole ranges of permanent security measures. Then too, police paperwork has increased, as Harold Wilson would say, 'exponentially', much of it as a result of cumbersome new statutes.

Finally, the police are harassed and hampered by a section of the media which reflects the anti-police culture of the middle-class intelligentsia. Newspapers such as the *Guardian*, *Independent* and *Observer*, and a number of current affairs and documentary programmes on both the BBC and ITV, often present the police as authoritarian, brutal, corrupt and lawless. No doubt the police do make mistakes, and they sometimes allow the mountain of difficulties they face in upholding the law to get the better of their tempers, with disastrous effects on their relations with the public. Police work is now extremely hazardous. Assaults on police, once rare, have multiplied a hundred times since the pre-war days, and policemen and even policewomen on duty are now often killed. That, too, helps to make the police tense and sometimes over-reactive. But they rightly resent attempts by a section of the media to present them as habitual enemies of the people, more particularly since they know that they enjoy, in general, the support and even the affection of ordinary citizens. The left-wing media attack on the police, helped by certain MPs and lawyers who have their own scores to settle, is another example of the way in which undemocratic groups operate to frustrate the will of the great majority in Britain.

All these factors, then, weaken law enforcement and demoralise those whose duty it is, Crown prosecutors as well as police. Crown prosecutors in particular, having limited budgets, are daunted by the way in which statute law now weights the scales of justice in favour of the offender. Often they drop cases which, a generation ago, would have been prosecuted with vigour and success. This has a devastating effect on public opinion in neighbourhoods where the crime is resented and the criminal known. Sometimes it forces the public to take the law into its own hands. In recent years lynch-mobs have been reported all over the country, but especially in traditional country districts, such as Anglesey, central Wales and East Anglia, where local community feeling is strong. Neighbourhoods have compensated for the powerlessness of the police by driving habitually criminal families from their midst. And there are a growing number of crimes of vengeance. Both forms of vigilanteism evoke popular approval, which can be tested by the verdicts of juries. A typical example occurred in Leeds in January 1994, when a Crown Court jury found not guilty a woman who had stabbed a man she believed had raped her four-year-old daughter. She had, she claimed, 'played it by the book' in reporting the offence to the police and cooperating with them in their investigations. The police were sure they had a case against the man but the Crown Prosecution Service, as often happens now, declined to proceed. At that point the woman lost confidence in the sytem of justice and attacked the man, who died as a result. The jury verdict indicated she had public opinion entirely on her side.

Can it be wondered at that the public feels it has a right to take action when the law manifestly fails? After all, systems of justice arise from a prescriptive compact between individuals and society to forgo personal vengeance in favour of collective retribution. When the collectivity fails, the moral right of vengeance returns to the individual. That is how ordinary people see it, and they have a point. Many people, particularly in areas of high crime rates – above all on crime-ridden housing estates – no longer report thefts, assaults or other crimes because they despair of the police bringing the perpetrators to book – or are sure that, if they do, the sentences will be derisory, or because they fear the criminals, or because it is simply too much trouble. The last was my reason for failing to report an attempted burglary by a thief whom I had surprised removing the window bars of my London house. He injured himself in making his get-away, and as he had succeeded in stealing nothing I decided to regard the matter as closed. My action, or inaction, may well have been antisocial but I believe many people these days would do the same. A progressive-minded friend, at about the same time, also failed to report two intruders whom he had surprised in his home after he had inadvertently left the front door open. He explained his behaviour to me by saying that he felt sorry for the men because they were black. So here, at an interval of a few days, were two cases, in the same district of London, where attempted burglaries or thefts went unreported. Anecdotal evidence – no other is available – suggests that the number of unreported crimes is now enormous. Hence the statistics of crime greatly underestimate its incidence. Bearing this in mind, we have every reason to be alarmed by the small number of reported crimes which are now solved. There was a time when between two-thirds and three-quarters of all crimes were cleared up by the police. Those days are long past. By 1980 the percentage of solved crimes had fallen to 36. The slow decline continued throughout the 1980s to 31 per cent in 1989. Since then there has been a sudden drop to 25 per cent in 1992 (at the time of writing 1993 figures are not yet available). The police still succeed, it appears, in solving more than three-quarters of violent offences and sex crimes. But in cases of burglary or theft from cars, the proportion is less than one in five. These are among the commonest of crimes and the ones most likely to impinge on the daily lives of most people. So the low success rate here gives the public the impression that the entire system of law enforcement is breaking down.

There is another factor which is undermining public confidence in the way order is maintained in Britain. People are accustomed to the rise of crime in the inner cities. Indeed some parts of London, such as Seven Dials, have been regarded as rookeries of crime for centuries. What has happened in the last decade, however, is that crime rates characteristic of inner cities have spread to suburban areas, or to small country towns or even to the countryside itself. Many professional criminals now operate not only in cities but in country districts, the motorway system providing their lines of communication and easy getaway. Figures released in the summer of 1993 demonstrated that it is traditionally conservative and rural areas like Wiltshire, Hampshire, Somerset and Dorset which now produce the most startling upward trends in crime, including violent crime. Country-dwellers now have to bolt and bar their houses as securely as those who live in central London, put alarms into their cars and avoid county towns on Friday and Saturday evenings. In the summer, entire rural districts, especially in Gloucestershire, Avon, parts of Somerset and the south Welsh borders, are terrorised by wandering bands of 'travellers' and 'New Age people', often thousands strong and contemptuous of the law. The police are often too few or too apprehensive to disperse them, let alone make arrests, and content themselves with 'moving on' these motorised convoys out of their districts. When these lawless bands camp for a spell, the only agents of authority which penetrate their defensive cordons are Social Security officials, who come to give them their weekly subsidies of taxpayers' money. Thus the public pays entire outlaw communities to harass farmers, destroy crops and hedges, steal from isolated houses and communities, block roads, create appalling sanitary problems and disturb the peace of law-abiding villages. It is not in the cities alone that belief in a just society is collapsing: in the heart of rural England, too, the tide of despair rises and erodes all ancient certitudes. In 1993 the Chief Constable of Manchester summed up the feelings of multitudes when he stated, flatly, 'Make no mistake; crime in Britain pays.' Ordinary men and women see that crime pays. They see, too, that Parliament takes little or no notice of their complaints or, perversely, passes new laws which make things even worse. And they therefore conclude, with bitterness and cynicism, that parliamentary democracy does not work in the land of its birth.

CHAPTER SIX

Mr, Mrs and Ms Sponge's Sporting Tour
of the Welfare State

For democracy to work, and be seen and felt to work, the people must be satisfied that their will is being respected on the points about which they care most passionately. They do not expect miracles. They know they cannot have good government for nothing. But they require reasonable obedience. Over a period, and on the central issues of policy, public desires, parliamentary enactments and government performance must be brought into rough alignment. That is not happening in Britain today. We have seen that on public order authority has lamentably failed to produce what the public wants and has a right to expect – an orderly society. The other central preoccupation of the public is getting and spending: the way in which government does its job and how it is paid for. Here too there has been a stunning failure on the part of Parliament and government, and a collapse in public confidence in the democratic process.

Revenue and expenditure is the heart of government, the very core of the parliamentary system. If Parliament fails there, it fails everywhere. And it is failing. Throughout the last millennium, the British people have shown again and again that the level and fairness of taxation is what they most care about in politics. They care about many other things from time to time. But taxation is their *idée fixe* of what government and politics is about. On the whole the British people combine a love of freedom and independence of mind with remarkable docility in paying taxes. Tax riots are very rare in British history. Tax evasion has probably been lower in this country than in any other. Even more remarkable, British tax collectors have never been mobbed or assaulted or murdered (it is another story with the Customs and Excise, a more aggressive branch of the executive). On the contrary, the taxing authorities in Britain are highly respected. The Treasury has always been held in public esteem. The Exchequer and its court were always bywords for honesty and punctiliousness. The Lords of the Treasury practised *noblesse oblige* and the Income Tax Commissioners, from their inception, were seen as stern but straightforward upper-middle-class gentlemen, anxious to do their duties to the general satisfaction. Whereas the 'publican' or tax collector was a figure of shame in the New Testament and has been held in hatred in most countries ever since, in Britain men and women are proud to work for the Inland Revenue.

The reason for this admirable state of affairs is that Parliament functioned effectively. It responded to public complaints; it saw that grievances were redressed. If taxes were too high, it lowered them. If the money raised was foolishly spent, it secured reform. It never let the Crown forget that it was the vigilant eye of the people, watching every penny spent. Even the magisterial Queen Elizabeth I was forced to bend to Parliament's will over public finance – and she was clever enough to do it with a good grace in her 'Golden Speech' of 1601. Charles I failed to heed all the warning signs and Parliament went to war with him over this very issue. It is perhaps not sufficiently realised how successful Parliament has been, over the centuries, in keeping the people sweet over public expenditure, and thus ensuring that Britain has been free from revolution.

A typical case of Parliament doing its democratic duty occurred at the end of the great wars against Bonapartist aggression. This had involved unprecedented levels of public expenditure, and so of taxation, including a horrific novelty – income tax. Sydney Smith, on behalf of the industrious classes, complained bitterly in the *Edinburgh Review* of the tax burden the wars imposed. The system, he wrote, slapped duties on every article which enters into the mouth, or covers the back, or is placed under the foot – taxes upon everything which is pleasant to see, hear, feel, smell or taste – taxes upon warmth, light and locomotion – taxes upon everything on earth and the waters under the earth – on everything that comes from abroad or is grown at home – taxes on the raw material – taxes on every fresh value that is added to it by the industry of man – taxes on the sauce that pampers man's appetite, and the drug that restores him to health – on the ermine which decorates the judge and the rope that hangs the criminal – on the poor man's salt and rich man's spice – on the brass nails of the coffin and the ribands of the bride – at bed or board, couchant or levant, we must pay – the schoolboy whips the taxed top – the beardless youth manages his taxed horse, with a taxed bridle, on a taxed road – and the dying Englishman, pouring his medicine which has paid 7 per cent, into a spoon that has paid 15 per cent, flings himself back on his bed, which has paid 22 per cent – and expires in the arms of an apothecary who has paid a license of £100 for the privilege of putting him to death. His whole property is then immediately taxed from 2 to 10 per cent – besides the probate, large fees are demanded for burying him in the chancel – his virtues are handed down to posterity on taxed marble – and he is then gathered to his fathers, to be taxed no more.

These feelings were widely shared, and there was particular anger against the new income tax, the most unpopular impost since the notorious Ship Money in Charles I's time. Members of Parliament who reflected the popular wrath saw it not merely as a monstrous burden but as an inquisitorial intrusion into the privacy of a man's financial affairs. Once the war was over they determined to get taxes down immediately and fundamentally, and abolish income tax for ever. In his great campaign against income tax in 1815–16, Henry Brougham produced evidence that income-tax returns had been sold as wastepaper and used to wrap cheese, so a customer might eat his Cheddar or Stilton and devour the financial secrets of a fellow citizen simultaneously. On 18 March 1816, in one of the most remarkable triumphs in Parliamentary history, and to the rage and terror of the government – whose customary majority was overwhelming – he succeeded in getting income tax abolished by a Commons majority of 238 to 201. He even demanded that all the records of 'this evil tax' be destroyed, so the secrets of how to levy and collect it would be denied to future governments. The crowds danced in the streets and the government had no alternative but to set about cutting its expenditure.

That is Parliament doing its job; and so it continued. After the First World War when taxation rose to heights even those who suffered the levels of Bonaparte's time would have found unimaginable, Parliament, responding to the popular will, succeeded in restoring reasonable levels. From the early 1920s to 1937 Britain enjoyed surprisingly modest levels of direct and indirect taxation, levels made possible because Parliament was vigilant and insistent, and government efficient and frugal. But it was a different story after the Second World War. Taxation never returned to pre-war levels. In some respects it increased. The principal reason for this was that the Labour Party, abandoning the populist attitudes of its radical predecessors, adopted policies of high expenditure and began to equate high taxation with public virtue. This was an astonishing turnabout, for the Tories had traditionally been the high-tax party, and Labour's conversion to profligacy meant that there was no powerful force in Parliament to lead the opposition to high spending and high taxing.

For half a century, then, ordinary wage-earners became accustomed – but never resigned – to surrendering from between a third and a half of their income in direct taxation. Some paid much more, for taxes on earned income went up to over 80 per cent and on so-called unearned income (i.e. savings) to over 90 per cent – and stayed there, indefinitely, as though part of the law of nature. Gradually, however, the Tories learned the lesson, and began to adopt low-taxation policies, at least in theory. They discovered what their predecessors had never needed to be taught from the fourteenth century on, that high taxes are unpopular. The great majority of the people, rich and poor, high and low, want taxes kept low; and if low taxation is insufficient to cover government expenditure, then they want expenditure reduced. This has been the central popular axiom of British politics for hundreds of years. And it has remained so in our own time. At every general election within living memory, in which voters have been able to distinguish a real difference between the parties in taxation policy and the curbing of public expenditure, they have given the victory to prudence. The success of the Conservatives in getting the public to recognise them as the party of (comparatively) low taxation explains why they have governed the country for thirty-six out of the last fifty years.

The Conservatives were much less successful in actually cutting public expenditure, and their programme of cutting taxes therefore remained nugatory until the 1980s. Under Margaret Thatcher, however, government and Parliament at last responded to public demand. The many higher-rate bands of income tax were abolished and reduced to one of 40 per cent. The basic rate was likewise reduced, to 25 and then 20 per cent. I recall a joyful conversation with Nigel Lawson, Margaret Thatcher's most ambitious Chancellor of the Exchequer, in which we jointly speculated on the possibility that, before the turn of the century, income tax could be reduced to almost nominal rates, indeed that direct taxation could be abolished altogether – thus recovering the pristine fiscal purity brought about by Henry Brougham in 1816.

But it was not to be. Even under Margaret Thatcher's stern and frugal eye, efforts to reduce expenditure substantially, either in aggregate or as a total of national income, met only limited success. She herself was discontented and bitter about her failure and complained to me on many occasions about the reluctance of government and Parliament to respond to the manifest public desire to get the cost of the state down. 'It is wicked' was the phrase she used, time and again. And it is. Gladstone warned repeatedly, throughout his long stewardship of the public finances, that unless the utmost vigilance was maintained at all times, public expenditure had an 'inherent' tendency to rise with 'overwhelming force': this constituted the 'greatest evil', the 'Original Sin' of government. Margaret Thatcher was likewise well aware that public overspending was not just wasteful but positively immoral, for all kinds of reasons, and she fought against it with passion. But she had many other dragons to slay and it may well be she devoted an insufficient proportion of her energies to this particular weakness of government. And when she was finally removed from office, by a conspiracy of big public spenders, many of the restraints she had succeeded in imposing on Whitehall profligacy began to be abandoned.

Of course in theory the Tories remained the low-tax party. They gloried in this role which they rightly recognised as their high-road to the voters' hearts. In the final stages of the 1992 election campaign, John Major exulted: 'Cutting taxes has been shown to be the greatest stimulus to economic growth and personal freedom there has ever been. Every pound we cut in tax is a pound more for people's choice, a pound more to create work for others, a pound more to buy things for the families. Apologise for that? Never! It is the greatest thing any government could do for the people. And when we win on Thursday there will be more of it!' The people believed him – or they gave him the benefit of the doubt. Or, rather, they believed accusations that, under Labour, taxes would rise. So they awarded the Conservatives, narrowly, a fourth spell in office. The 1992 elections showed conclusively that even a manifestly tired party that has been in government for many years, has done many foolish things and is led by a man of feeble qualifications and uncertain merits, can secure another mandate if the voters are persuaded it will give them lower taxes than the alternative parties.

Yet, at the beginning of 1994, the people are ruefully aware that democracy has failed them again. Having avoided the Labour Scylla in 1992, they foundered on the Tory Charybdis. Expenditure has not been curbed. Borrowing has risen to a prodigious £50 billion a year – nearly a billion a week – and taxes are rising again. In his New Year message, Major sounded a far more defensive note than in his election-eve address. He admitted he had had to 'raise revenue' and pleaded in extenuation he had 'not put up income-tax rates'. He no longer felt able to claim that Conservatism was 'the party of low taxation'. What he said was: 'The Conservative Party remains the party of the lowest possible tax, the party of low income tax and the only party whose instinct is to cut tax.' Even this was soon demonstrated to be untrue. A financial study by *The Times*, later confirmed by Treasury figures, showed that, taking into account the two budgets of 1993, personal taxation in the current year is higher than in 1979, the last year of Labour rule. The Chancellor of the Exchequer himself, it calculated, would have paid approximately 20 per cent of his income in direct tax in 1979; in 1993/4 he will be paying approximately 30 per cent. The autumn Budget of 1993 raised taxation, direct and indirect, in a variety of ways ingeniously contrived to camouflage the real impact. The Labour Party argued when the Budget was first published that it would cost the average British family an extra £10 a week in tax, and that it was the biggest tax-increase budget in thirty years. Detailed Treasury figures available by early 1994 show this was an underestimate. The Budget has emerged as probably the most onerous in peacetime history, which will cost a married couple with two children and one earner on average earnings of £19,450 a year an extra £12.52 a week.

The undemocratic nature of the 1993 budgets can be displayed in other ways. The Tory presentation of itself as the low-tax party centred on its defence of the family – it was families, especially young families, Conservative spokesmen argued, who benefited from their tax policies. That was in line with what the public undoubtedly wanted: a low tax burden on all, but especially on families with children. Treasury studies show, however, that exactly the opposite is now happening. Whereas in 1979 families had to fork out 32.2 per cent of their income in tax, in the financial year beginning in April 1994 the percentage will rise to 35 per cent. And by 1995/6, by which time more of the projected increases will come into effect, the tax burden of the average family will rise to a colossal 35.9 per cent, the highest in British history.

How has this savage financial assault on the typical British family – this negation of theoretical Tory policy – this undemocratic defiance of what the public wants and is universally known to want – come about? The answer can be given in four words; failure to cut expenditure – indeed, failure to stop expenditure rising. And why has this failure occurred?

Because Parliament lacked the will to carry out the nation's wishes. Because it listened to the lobbies, the pressure groups, the 'experts', the know-all academics, the unions, the professional associations – to everybody, in fact, except the people. The results are absolutely damning. Under Margaret Thatcher, there was an 18.3-per-cent real rise in government spending over twelve years (that is, 1978/9 to 1990/91). Under John Major there will, on the plans at the time of writing, be a 15.4-per-cent increase over six years (1990/91 to 1996/7). The average annual rise in real terms under Mrs Thatcher was thus 1.4 per cent and under Major is 2.4 per cent. In the last three years alone public spending has risen a huge 12 per cent in real terms. The Tories, just as much as Labour, are a high-spending party.

With all the special interests claiming their spending is uncuttable, the total projected outgoings of central government in 1994 amount to £251,300 million. Quite obscure departments now swallow up money reckoned in billions. Thus, the Lord Chancellor's department runs off with £3.4 billion, the Foreign Office requires £1.2 billion, National Heritage nearly a billion, the Environment another billion, the Population Census £1.3 billion, the government legal departments £2.7 billion and so on. But these are peanuts compared with the big spenders. The 'Celtic periphery', Scotland, Wales and Northern Ireland, now swallows up £28,150 million – over £5 billion more than the entire cost of national defence. Then there are the two hugely overmanned areas, Health and the portion of the vast cost of local government covered by central taxation, which together amount to £72,650 million. However, the biggest single item on the entire list, amounting to well over a quarter of the whole, is Social Security at £79,000 million.

Gladstone once warned that, when public expenditure got out of control, it followed, 'as night follows day', that fraud and corruption would occur on a colossal scale too. He was thinking in terms of hundreds, perhaps thousands of pounds. Now the criminal element, or the criminally wasteful element, totals scores of billions. To begin with, the Treasury itself fails to collect large sums from tax-evaders – itself a sure symptom of an overtaxed society. Uncollected tax stood at £4.3 billion in

1991, enough to pay for what we spend on agriculture and trade and industry put together. It has since been reduced, but only by writing off billions classified as 'unrecoverable'. Then there are the 'Professor Brainstorm experiments'. In January 1994 the National Audit Office revealed that £42 million of public money had been irrecoverably lost in what was called the Geothermal Hot Dry Rocks Project. This absurd scheme finally concluded, after the money had been spent, that 'electricity cannot be generated at competitive prices by this method in the foreseeable future'. And this wild project was approved by Parliament without dissent and without any consultation with the voters. The same month, the Commons Public Accounts Committee, a body which draws attention to wasteful expenditure of money which Parliament should never have voted in the first place, reported that virtually all the major Whitehall departments had been affected by falling standards in probity and efficiency in the two years 1992 and 1993. Thus the Department of Employment had lost £55 million in 'doubtful and incorrect payments' to Training and Enterprise Councils and private companies. It had wasted £48 million on a computer system giving 'poor value for money'. The accounting services of the Foreign Office had 'created a climate which was conducive to fraud and theft'. The Property Services Agencies, in charge of all Whitehall real estate, had lost £56.6 million because its accounting system had 'broken down'. The Ministry of Defence had actually contrived to launch an 'efficiency savings scheme' by giving a series of lavish parties involving unauthorised expenditure.

Much of the money lost or stolen, according to the National Audit Office and the Commons Accounts Committee, is attributable to quangos. These are bureaucratic monsters familiar from the worst days of Labour rule in the 1970s, now enjoying a new and vigorous lease of life. The quango, or Quasi-Autonomous Non-Governmental Organisation, is by its nature inclined to be undemocratic because it lives in a no-man's-land beyond the formal premises of Whitehall departments. In theory it is supervised by Parliament but in practice it often carries on absorbing substantial sums of public money without most people knowing it even exists. It is characteristic of the mist which envelops quangoland that I have never been able, at any one time, to get an accurate official figure for the total number of quangos. Nor has anyone else. All kinds of figures have been quoted. It is said that, under James Callaghan, the total exceeded 2000 and that it was then reduced by Margaret Thatcher, who hated quangos, to a mere 800. Something like this may be true. It is now said – I write of reports circulating early in 1994 – that because of the Thatcherite policy of hiving off parts of government departments into semi-autonomous agencies, a scheme introduced to raise efficiency and save money, the number of quangos has again jumped, to 2100, and that by the end of 1996, when this devolvement is complete, they will form a grand total of 8000. Already, it is said (but no one seems to know), quangos account for the spending of £42 billion, about a fifth of all expenditure. By the end of 1996 they will, it is said, be spending £55 billion.

It is a practical axiom of our parliamentary system of government that the people who decide how money is to be raised are MPs, elected by voters, and that the people in charge of spending it are either ministers or civil servants. The ministers must themselves be Members of Parliament and answerable directly to it. The civil servants are chosen by competitive examination and their conditions of service governed by strict rules which Parliament minutely supervises, at least in theory. That is all as it should be. But quangos are run, and often staffed, by a third and entirely different category of person. The quango-monger is not elected by anyone. He is not required by law to have qualifications. He can indeed be Tom, Dick or Harry, or Caroline, Sarah or Jane. What he or she does require is government patronage. Quangoland is an enormous, totally undemocratic system of outdoor relief for the good, the great and the well-befriended. I do not doubt that many who serve on quangos deserve to be there. It is equally beyond question that many others are the unworthy beneficiaries of a lax and unsupervised system which provides jobs, often powerful and well-paid jobs, for the boys and girls who, for one reason or another, enjoy the favour of ministers. Certain categories of people get their snouts stuck in the quango trough, depending on which government is in power. Thus in the late 1970s, when Labour was dispensing the jobs, the commonest recipients of seats on plum quangos were trade union barons. I discovered that one such baron sat on no fewer than thirteen quangos and since he was also in supposedly full-time employment by his union there was a distinct flavour of sinecurism about his appointments. Under the Conservatives, a lot of nice quangos go to busybody businessmen, the sort of 'executives' who do not find employment at the top of big, highly-competitive companies – they are not good enough – but who love to sit on committees. Under both Labour and Conservatives, quango jobs also go in great quantity to academics – the sort of academics who do not notably expand the frontiers of knowledge but who are assiduous explorers of the byways of Westminster and Whitehall.

The way in which quangoland and the quango-mongers militate against democracy can be seen in the case of London. In 1993 the London boroughs were democratically represented by 1975 councillors, all directly elected. But a survey by the London *Evening Standard* showed that only thirty-five of them sat on or played any part in London's vast range of quangos. For instance, London's four regional health authorities, which were responsible for spending over £5.5 billion in 1993, have no elected men or women on their boards, nor have the district health authorities which report to them. The London Docklands Development Corporation, which spent £186 million in 1993, includes only three councillors on its board, and there are only two on the London Pension Funds authority, which spent £244 million in 1993. London's housing action trusts are the most democratic, in that half their board members are drawn from local councils. But this is exceptional. The boards of London's technology colleges are appointed entirely by central government – nothing democratic about them. That is typical. Altogether, London's quangos spent over £6 billion in 1993 and democratic representation on them was minute.

Nobody is saying that the people who run quangos are corrupt or even particularly inefficient. But obviously the less accountable a body spending public money is – or the more remote its accountability – the less likely it is that mistakes and frauds will be detected before the cash goes down the drain. And that is exactly what experience shows. The Commons Public Accounts Committee, reporting early in 1994, made some damning observations, for instance, about the West Midlands Regional Health Authority. It concluded that one director should have been dismissed for appointing consultants without following the rules. (At the time of writing, police are investigating this matter.) There were 'very serious failings' at all levels of management, resulting in the waste of £10 million. An even worse case was the Wessex Regional Health Authority, accused by the Committee of 'grave shortcomings', 'conceal-ment of vital information', conflicts of interest, waste and mismanagement, as a result of which £20 million was wasted. Another bad case was the Treasury's own catering quango, where the Committee found malpractice and fraud, poor control, mismanagement and various irregularities. A number of Welsh quangos came in for severe criticism. The Welsh Development Agency, for instance, appointed to a senior position a man described by the Committee as a 'crook' with 'forged references'. (Police investigations are afoot in Welsh quangoland, too.)

However, when all the various frauds, mismanagements and examples of waste in Whitehall departments and central and local quangos are added together, it is most improbable the total would exceed, or even come close to, the frauds and fiddles imposed on the Department of Social Security and its offshoots. It doles out close to £80 billion a year and how much of this is, in effect, stolen by fraudsters and impostors is anyone's guess. A billion? Five billion? Twenty billion? It could well be the last figure. The commonest form of fraud is committed by countless recipients of social security who are, in fact, making a living through self-employment or who actually hold regular jobs. But there is a great deal of systematic, organised fraud too. Britain is notorious throughout the world as operating a social security system which makes it easy for criminals. Certain nationalities specialise in defrauding the British taxpayers. First into the field, needless to say, were the Irish, who flock across the Irish Sea in great numbers to exploit Britain's welfare state, which they regard as a kind of patriotic duty.

When Richard Crossman was Secretary of State for Social Security, he told me that it was skilled and voluble Irish mendicants, hanging around welfare offices, who had first corrupted and instructed the Caribbeans in the art of social security fraud. The Caribbeans, in turn, passed the word to West African immigrants and visitors, who proved apt pupils. Indeed some of the largest and most prolonged social security robberies, involving millions of pounds of false claims a week, have been carried out by gangs of West Africans, men and women, masterminded from Lagos, Accra and other African capitals. The latest recruits to the business come from the European Community, whose nationals, especially Spanish, Greeks, Portuguese and Italians, rejoice in the easy opportunities for large-scale deceptions. Visitors from southern Italy and Sicily, as perhaps one might expect, are particularly skilful at extracting social security funds from gullible officials.

But when all is said and done, the bulk of the vast sums swallowed by social security does not go to crooks. The truth is, the system was designed to be profligate. Or, rather, it was designed to put helping the 'needy', irrespective of their moral worth, before every other consideration, including above all financial prudence. To begin with, the system is grossly overstaffed, employing a vast army of over 700,000 people. Its maxim seems to be that it is better to have too many handing out the cash than to risk one solitary person 'in need' going without. That is one reason why the social security authorities are so anxious to set up emergency handout centres, notoriously prodigal in manpower, to serve what they call their 'customers' among the New Age travellers and other sturdy beggars. This vast system of outdoor relief to the idle and indigent operates, generally speaking, according to the rules. The rules may infuriate the vast majority of ordinary taxpayers, but they were laid down by Parliament and are administered by, on the whole, conscientious officials. It is MPs who are ultimately responsible for creating what is, properly considered, an evil system, a true opium of the people, which creates welfare addicts and introduces originally innocent people into a culture of dependence and hopeless lassitude. It turns decent people into parasites and callous exploiters of the industrious. In the autumn of 1993, some government ministers, alarmed by reports that one in three births in Britain were illegitimate, and that a large and growing proportion of these single mothers and their offspring were now entirely dependent on social security, began a campaign of exhortations and feeble administrative measures to curtail the abuse. Half-hearted as it was, it instantly ran into vociferous abuse from the powerful and well-financed welfare lobbies. Ministers, accused of cruelty and heartlessness, quickly began to backtrack, even before one of their number was found guilty of adding to the illegitimate population himself. It is obvious that many of these single mothers are sad and pitiful cases, and no one in gainful employment wants to deny them their pittance. It is equally obvious that the system is exploited by countless young women and their boyfriends, who see no shame at all in getting what cash they can from the state. Cases of abuse which come to light, and are publicised in the tabloids, are dismissed by the welfare lobbies and pressure groups as 'anecdotal evidence'. But the overall statistics are equally eloquent of gross abuse. And, in any case, there is a lot to be said for anecdotal evidence. It is the basis on which most of us go through life forming judgments; it always has been and always will be. Anecdotal evidence is the raw material of experience. We vote on the basis of anecdotal evidence, and it is because we hear of cases, and ponder them, that we decide whether our political system – our democracy – is working, and usually conclude it is not.

What strikes one particularly about cases of abuse is that the beneficiaries regard their conduct as reasonable, normal and entirely blameless. That is the way they have been conditioned by society. They are mostly young people and they know no other life. It would be as pointless to appeal to their consciences as it would be to tell them that listening to Mahler and Beethoven is a more rewarding experience than staying tuned to continuous pop music. I was intrigued by a recent minor court case from Cornwall, in which one competitor for the title of Miss Tin Mine 1993 was accused by another of giving her a black eye, and tipping her mother into a flowerbed. The evidence gave a fascinating glimpse into the workings of the provincial beauty-queen industry, in which both girls had spent their entire lives. One had won over 2000 trophies though she was only fourteen. The other was also highly successful, and older: twenty-two, in fact. The account, almost as a footnote, recorded that she had three illegitimate children already and that all four were living on social security while she pursued her life as a professional beauty.

A still more revealing case, because it lent itself to calculation as to its cost to the public, was a woman from Yorkshire, who has eleven children, nine of them illegitimate. So far as one could discover this woman has never been in gainful employment or contributed one penny to her own subsistence or that of her offspring. The nine bastards are by the same father, and he too had contributed nothing, 'not a penny' as he proudly put it; he too was unemployed and 'on benefit'. The case came to light because public anger had been aroused among locals waiting for council houses by news that the woman was to be given three council houses, knocked into one at considerable public expense. The local council, Kirklees near Huddersfield, calculated that it was cheaper to do this than to put the woman and her children 'into accommodation', at a hotel or boarding-house. They were also, it appeared, providing her with what was described as 'live-in home help and back-up' at a cost of £50,000 a year. Naturally, local people who had led blameless and industrious lives were furious that the woman's irresponsibility should be rewarded by a free and spacious house, servants and maintenance. She herself saw nothing unusual in the arrangements, saying that these were her 'rights' and blaming 'press intrusion' for the fuss. The council was blamed, but it is arguable that it was simply carrying out its statutory obligations, imposed on it and all other councils by Act of Parliament – an act, needless to say, demanded not by the voters but pushed through by pressure groups and welfare lobbies. However, the real sting is in the tail – the financial bottom line. The cost to the public of the needs of this woman and her children in 1994 (while the housing work is being carried out) will be £196,580, the equivalent of the total taxes paid by sixty working people on average wages; thereafter, in 1995 and beyond, of forty working people.

This kind of calculation is extremely illuminating, because it reveals the burden, in purely human terms, of sustaining a welfare system which has got completely out of control, which is financially unsustainable in the long run – increasingly so even in the short run, as 1993's record borrowings make clear – which is itself a great moral evil in the way it corrupts its recipients, and which is fundamentally undemocratic because it is despised and repudiated by the mass of the people. Taking into account all its many baroque forms, the system is now increasingly producing what might be called 'welfare millionaires', irresponsible and heedless people each of whom can cost the public cumulative sums running into millions. I know of one woman, herself on social security – she has always been on social security so far as I am aware – who has produced a number of offspring, by various fathers. They have had to be placed in local authority boarding schools run for 'disturbed children' (that is, children who, because of their upbringing or lack of it, have become incorrigibly naughty). These are the most expensive schools in the country, probably in Europe: to send a child there costs more than to send him or her to Eton or Cheltenham Ladies College. I calculate that this one woman has already cost taxpayers more than a million pounds and will probably get through another million before she is finished. Lloyd George, campaigning for his famous radical budget of 1909, took a series of pot-shots at dukes, who were opposing his finance bill in the House of Lords. Dukes, he claimed, 'cost more than battleships'. The calculation has now been upended. Today we have indigent women who cost more than dukes. And, whereas there are only, at the latest count, twenty-six dukes, the number of such women is, in theory, limitless.

The failure of Parliament to control the welfare state, by reducing it to a common-sense system of help for those who really need it, is the greatest of all Parliamentary failures. Taken in conjunction with the failure to control taxation – the two of course are connected – it reveals Parliament, over a generation or more, as an institution which has betrayed the interests and disregarded the wishes of the people. The financial irresponsibility of Parliament – I use irresponsible in both senses of the word – over the past generation or so is unique in its long history and is the aspect of the democratic breakdown in Britain which most urgently needs to be put right. Gladstone rightly observed that, in a free country, financial control is the best, the speediest, the surest and in the long run the only effective form of control. If Parliament has the strength of will to cut off the funds, all those who disregard the public's wishes, or who feel themselves to be above the rules of democratic supervision, will be brought to heel. The wasters, the corrupt, the incompetents, the arrogant, the self-righteous, the holier-than-thou enthusiasts who try to build utopia on earth with other people's money – all these pests who infest the entrails of an overfed and obese modern government – cannot function without their salaries and their departmental budgets. Cut these budgets, better still abolish them, and the pests are helpless to do harm.

However financial control, though essential, is not enough. To become an instrument of democracy again, Parliament must reassert positive policy control too. We have seen how power has slipped out of its hands over the whole spectrum of crime and its punishment. But there are other areas of almost equal importance and public concern, where the lobbies and the pressure groups have taken over. The most obvious of these is education. It is hard to think of any subject where the divergence between what the public wants, and what the state provides, is greater. The demands of ordinary people are not exorbitant. They want all children to read, to read easily, accurately and sustainedly; to form, if possible, the habit of reading and acquire the taste for good literature. They want all children to be taught to write, legibly, fluently and grammatically, to acquire a reasonably wide vocabulary and to spell correctly. They want all children to be numerate and to handle proficiently the elementary instruments of a modern electronic society. Children, they think, should be taught about their country's history and geography, to the point where they grasp the peculiar nature of Britain and its institutions, and learn to value its qualities. They want children to acquire in school, reinforcing home training, habits of diligence, punctuality, neatness, cleanliness and civility. And, not least, they want the schools to provide, for all children, a moral education: to instil, not just directly and specifically, but through all the school structures and procedures, clear distinctions between right and wrong, good and evil, decent behaviour and wickedness.

This is not a great deal to ask from a well-run school, and it is all parents ask, as of right, for their children. Of course they hope for more. They expect their children to be educated according to their abilities and to climb the ladder right to university and beyond if they have the skill and industry. Most people do not ask for equality except of opportunity, because they have the sense to know that all other kinds are chimerical. They liked, for instance, the old grammar schools, many of which went back to the sixteenth century and were the pride of their neighbourhoods. They value the scholarship system, at all levels. They favour the assisted-places schemes, which enable children from poor or modest homes to go to the best schools in the country, including boarding schools, getting there on their own merits. They see secondary and tertiary education as a highly competitive business, rightly so, in which children get to the top and acquire valuable qualifications because they are naturally bright and work hard. All the instincts of the people are to use education as the means to create a true meritocracy.

In fact what Parliament has allowed to emerge, over the past half-century, is an educational system which might have been designed to produce a mobocracy. I will not dwell here on the large numbers of young people who now leave school virtually illiterate and innumerate, because the figures are well known, and government and Parliament, to a limited extent and very late in the day, are actually doing something to improve matters. But it is worth pausing to consider the combination of factors which produced a state education system which has provided less and less while costing more and more. Essentially they are twofold: trade unionism and ideology. One of the cleverest of our Secretaries of State for Education in recent years once remarked to me: 'The biggest single enemy of decent education in this country is the National Union of Teachers.' This was once a very powerful union and still has considerable destructive capacity. It has always been geared to represent the interests of the least qualified, least intelligent and least industrious members of the teaching profession and has in practice directed its energies to ensuring that its members do the least possible work for the highest possible pay. It also propagates among its members, and publicly supports, the latest 'progressive' nostrums, provided they fit in with its primary aim. All that is perfectly lawful, and the NUT (and indeed the other teachers' organisations, which are only slightly less reprehensible) is no more selfish and destructive in its aims than any other trade organisation formed to advance the interests of a particular group of people. The political and moral blame lies with successive governments, formed from successive parliaments, which have permitted the NUT, and the other unions, so large a say in how we educate our children.

They have done so because the political and professional climate in which education policy is made favours rule by 'community' rather than democracy. The Department of Education has for many decades been controlled by ideologues and social engineers who believe that an egalitarian and what they would call 'just' society can be brought into existence by manipulating children in school. These people are in intimate contact – indeed they often exchange roles – with those who run the teacher-training colleges, the education faculties of universities, the schools inspectorate, trade papers like the *Times Educational Supplement*, the *Times Higher Educational Supplement* and so forth, and who serve as education correspondents for the principal newspapers. The components of Britain's 'education community' have their own internal schisms and bickerings, but they are at one in believing that education policy and practice should be decided by the 'experts' and not by the ordinary people.

So where does this leave the ordinary people? They pay their taxes, contributing to what is in real terms the largest educational budget in our history, and all they expect in return is that their children and grandchildren should get the kind of education which gives them a fair start in a meritocratic society. But it is very much a matter of luck whether they get it. Thanks to social engineering, and the *carte blanche* it gives local-authority education bureaucrats and teachers to pursue the principle in practice, state schools vary enormously in quality. Dependable standards have vanished. The wealthy contract out of the state system altogether. So do conscientious parents of modest means who put their children's education before every other form of expenditure. Some parents – a growing number – change their homes and even their jobs to establish residence qualifications in a district where there is a good state school. Thus the unscrupulous dogmatism of the 'experts' is to some extent compensated for by the individual heroism of families. But most parents have no choice but to take what the state and the 'experts' offer, and it is frequently very bad indeed.

Can they exert political pressure to get improvements, or a return to former standards? They can try. But until recently the 'education community' has succeeded in effecting a cross-party consensus which allowed policy to remain very much in the hands of the Department's social engineers. As members of Labour governments, Anthony Crosland and Shirley Williams were egregiously bad Education Secretaries who together destroyed the grammar-school system as a pillar of fair-minded meritocracy. But Margaret Thatcher, as Ted Heath's Education Secretary in 1970–74, was only marginally better. Not until the second half of the 1980s, very late in the day indeed, did Conservative ministers begin to break up the 'expert' consensus and seek to reimpose minimal standards, by bringing in a national curriculum, regular testing and compulsory levels of attainment, as well as by allowing local communities to opt out of local government control and run their own state schools. But these attempts to break away from the old, failed system of dogma and theory have been patchy, half-hearted and often confused, leading to much disruption and bitter arguments. There has been far too little consultation with the people, and the results, to date at least, have been meagre.

In the meantime, the people have to pay huge sums for a state education system which they know is a gamble. The worst off are the very poor. For it is in the areas where they live that ideologically-motivated education, provided by over-whelmingly left-wing Labour councils, is most like to occur. All the most flagrant excesses of classroom social engineering have come to light in the inner cities. There, parents have to be content with small mercies. A fascinating example of what parents put up with occurred in the poor London borough of

Hackney in 1993. One of its schools had been notorious for poor teaching and disorder. Things had much improved under a new headmistress called Jane Brown. She ruled with a firm hand, and the parents were grateful. But Ms Brown is a lesbian. Her predilections were uncovered when she prevented her pupils accepting the offer of free seats at a ballet of *Romeo and Juliet* on the grounds that it was an unbalanced presentation of heterosexual love. Uproar followed when the London *Evening Standard* publicised the story. Her refusal was seen as an extreme and reprehensible example of political correctness as well as a genuflexion towards her own sexual bias, and there was more trouble when it was suggested that her lesbian lover, a school governor, had helped to secure her appointment. But the more public-spirited of the parents objected strongly to plans to suspend or remove her. They were furious about the ballet business and obviously unhappy about her lesbianism. But at least she was making it possible for their children to get a bit of education. They were learning to read and write and calculate. Truancy in the school was down. Discipline was much improved. For a state school in a poor neighbourhood in the Britain of 1994 that was indeed something to be grateful for, and the parents were happy to settle for it. This sad little tale, indeed, tells us a lot about the failure of democracy in our country.

One final point, while we are on the subject of the refusal of the members of the House of Commons to do what the people who send them there want. From its inception, the redressing of grievances by petition and reform was one of the prime functions of Parliament. It ought to be so today. And there is no shortage of grievances, most of them arising from the activities of officious bureaucrats in central and local government. For some years now Christopher Booker of the *Sunday Telegraph* has been drawing attention to the growing mass of regulations affecting virtually every aspect of our national life, but especially the wealth-producing process on which we all depend; to the illogicalities, contradictions and labyrinthine insanities of these rules; and to the damage they do to the economy and indeed to the lives of the ordinary people. His activities have made him much hated and feared in Whitehall. He has been

doing, in fact, what Parliament ought to be doing, and doesn't
do. And of course almost the first thing he discovered was that
the principal culprit, in producing the rules, was Parliament
itself. It was Parliament which passed such noxious pieces of
bureaucratic regulation as the Health and Safety At Work Act
1974, itself progenitor of the Control Of Substances Hazardous
To Health Regulations 1988, the Electricity At Work Regulations 1988, and the Manual Handling, Visual Display Screens,
Personal Protective Equipment And Provision And Use Of
Work Equipment Regulations 1992; the Financial Services Act
1986, the Consumer Protection Act 1987, progenitor of the
Furniture And Furnishings Regulations 1988, the Toy Safety
Regulations 1989, the Weighing Machines Regulations 1988,
the Food Imitations Regulations 1989 and the Price Marketing
Regulations 1991; the Children's Act 1989 and the Community
Care Act 1990; the Environmental Protection Act 1990,
progenitor of the Waste Management Regulations 1991, the
Environmental Protection (Proscribed Processes And
Substances) Regulations 1991, and others too numerous to
mention; the Water Resources Act 1991 and its attendant
regulations; the Food Safety Act 1990, progenitor of three
enormous sets of regulations and many minor ones; plus a huge
mass of European Community regulations incorporated by
Parliament into English law and dealing with the minutiae of
the collection of VAT and such aspects of the Common
Agricultural Policy as 'set-aside', 'cattle passports', 'plant
passports', 'IACS', 'beef premium', 'sheep quota' and countless regulations affecting fish, fishing, fishermen, fishing nets,
fishing boats and fishy smells. Members of Parliament, supposedly the redressers of grievances, passed laws making
possible these regulations in most cases not knowing what they
were voting for or why, let alone the ultimate consequences of
their votes on ordinary people, but simply trudging through the
voting lobbies at the behest of the whips, who themselves had
little idea of what was afoot. (I recently asked the Chief Whip
whether he had grasped what would be the political consequences of introducing the Child Support Agency, for which
Parliament voted in its sleep. 'No,' he replied, 'I had absolutely
no idea.')

In February 1994, Christopher Booker, assisted by Richard North, produced a book of case-histories arising from this mass of statutes and regulations, *The Mad Officials: How the Bureaucrats are Strangling Britain* (Constable £7.95). These 140 instances present a nightmare picture of how Stalinist-minded officials have effectively escaped from the control of ministers and Parliament and are now choking to death British firms and individuals. It is riveting reading for anyone with a strong stomach. Booker's campaign has, of course, proved extremely popular with the general public, and especially with businesses, large and small. It has therefore caused the government some trouble, and early in 1994 they produced their response: the Deregulation Bill. This in itself was a monster; a statute of 106 pages plus 300 pages of 'supporting documents'. But it was put together by the Cabinet's leading conjuror, Michael Heseltine, and it turns out to be a mere public-relations trick. Booker's own analysis shows that it consists of seven elements: (1) repealing a mass of obsolete trivia, such as the Pedlars Act 1871; (2) deferment or rejection of measures the government had no intention of introducing anyway; (3) issuing 'starter packs' and leaflets to explain regulations; (4) 'abolishing' regulations it had already decided could not be made to work at all; (5) promising to 'press the EC' to allow Britain to water down its directives (some hope!); (6) further promises to keep objectionable regulations 'under review'; (7) the neatest con-juring trick of all – a promise to set about 'deregulation' by setting up a series of new regulatory bodies to monitor the rules.

The net effect of this fraudulent bill will be to create more jobs for officials. The truth is, as any intelligent person who has observed bureaucrats at work knows, the only way to control them is to reduce their numbers. Sacked officials cannot enforce regulations or issue new ones. Without real blood – masses of it – on the floors of Whitehall, no deregulation bill is going to work. And this bill promises no blood at all. To reassure the civil service unions, it goes out of its way to point out that it 'will have minimal or no effect on public service manpower'. In other words: carry on bureaucrats, all your jobs are safe.

So, the House of Commons is failing democracy. Under the present ministerial guidance it plainly intends to go on failing.

What of the longstop of our legislature, the 'revising chamber' or the House of Lords? Is any democracy stirring there? We shall have a look.

CHAPTER SEVEN

The House of Lords:
a Masterpiece of Sleazy Privilege

All systems of representative government have a directly-elected first chamber whose primary purpose is to raise money and initiate legislation. The majority also have second chambers which have a variety of functions, from revision of new bills to providing geographical balance. The most success-ful and highly esteemed is the US Senate, which has a regional basis and massive powers. Its members are directly elected for six years in two-year rotations and they enjoy great prestige precisely because in most cases their electorates are vast. A senator for California or New York state is chosen by more people than elect presidents in many countries. Second chambers elsewhere in the world have fewer powers as a rule, but all possess some by virtue of their representative nature. All contain a directly or indirectly elective element, which in most is predominant or entire.

The notorious exception is Britain's House of Lords. On close inspection it is seen to perform no function other than to demonstrate that the British do not take democracy seriously. It is sometimes said to 'work very well', but the people expressing this view are invariably those who already are or hope to become members of it. The functional efficiency of the House of Lords is a myth. As a revising chamber it is no use at all precisely because it has no real powers. A true second chamber should be able to restrain the financial profligacy or the legislative over-enthusiasm of the first chamber. The Lords can do neither. It lost its right to block new and outrageous taxes eighty years ago, before the First World War. At the same time its legislative function was reduced to a mere delaying power of two years, reduced to one year after the Second World War. By negotiating informally with the government of the day it sometimes improves a bill, but just as often it emasculates one.

Its record in recent years has been appalling. All the massive, oppressive, bureaucratic and anti-democratic statutes of the 1980s were given an easy ride in the Lords. It did nothing to mitigate the more absurd provisions of the Children's Act 1989 – including the right of children to 'divorce' their parents – or to question the so-called 'Criminals' Charter', the Criminal Justice Act 1991. The public protests which led to changes in this infamous Act occurred not because of but despite the Lords, which gave it a hearty welcome. If the House of Lords is intended to be a democratic longstop, as some claim, it is no good at all. Every ball hurled by the bureaucrats and the lobbies gets through.

The Lords cannot be entrusted with real powers for the simple reason that none of its members has a popular mandate. The preamble to the 1911 Parliament Act which reduced its powers to a delaying function declared: 'It is intended to substitute for the House of Lords as it at present exists a Second Chamber constituted on a popular instead of a hereditary basis.' More than eighty years later, nothing has been done to carry out this intention, an indication of the sustained lack of interest among Britain's ruling elites in making democracy work. All members of the Lords are there not as representatives but as persons, each receiving an individual writ of summons. The constitutional assumption underlying this procedure is that each peer has a definite personal contribution to make to the good governance of the realm. In the later Middle Ages, this made sense because the House of Lords was a small and select assembly of 150 members or less, each of whom was a major landowner. It was the natural successor to the earlier Great Council of the Realm, consisting of the monarch's tenants-in-chief who held their lands of him by knight-service, and thus provided the bulk of the nation's defences. Although its members were divided into Lords Spiritual and Lords Temporal, the archbishops, bishops, abbots and priors were also present primarily as landowners, who provided military contingents or money in lieu.

Today the House of Lords is a large, unwieldy body of about 1200 who could not conceivably be accommodated in their chamber if all attended at once. Nearly all are old, some very old: Clement Attlee appointed one peer aged 94. Most of them are hereditary peers, there simply because a distant or recent forebear held wide estates, performed some notable service to the nation or was adept at operating the system. Their only qualification is that they be aged twenty-one or over, are not aliens, lunatics, bankrupts or criminals serving sentences, and can prove they are the heir to a peer, now deceased, who attended by individual writ. A few are indeed landlords on a large scale but they are, oddly enough, the least likely to attend regularly as they have better things to do. They turn up mainly to take part in specific votes, such as on leasehold reform, in order to defend their personal interests. Other rich hereditary peers, with substantial business interests, treat the House of Lords in the same way. The heads of the great political landed families, whose ancestors played notable parts in British history – the Cecils, the Cavendishes, the Stanleys, the Bentincks, the Petty-Fitzmaurices, the Howards and so forth – are still members of the Lords and may even participate in some debates, but now play only a very marginal part in politics. Some Scottish and Irish noblemen, who do not hold English peerages, are elected as 'representative' peers of their country – by their fellow peers, of course, not by the public – and therefore feel a moral obligation to attend, at any rate when Scottish or Ulster matters are before the House. But even they are often absentees, if their means are ample and their duties and pleasures many.

The bulk of the hereditary peers who attend regularly do so for two reasons only: to collect their daily attendance fee (now £31, plus various accommodation and travel expenses, when incurred) and to avail themselves of their membership privileges. The House of Lords has often been described as 'the best club in the world'. Costing £39.5 million annually, it is certainly one of the most expensive to maintain. It has a magnificent library and reading room, bars, a restaurant and many other facilities, all of them for the use of peers and (where appropriate) their wives and families. It is not quite true to say there is no entrance fee, since newly-joining peers are mulcted of large sums by various heralds and other ancient flunkeys, but this money is pocketed by the officials concerned and none of it goes back to the taxpayer. Apart from this, there is no annual subscription; on the contrary, the Lords is the only club in the world where members are paid to turn up.

As a result, the hereditary peers most likely to attend the Lords regularly are men of modest means or even the indigent, for whom the daily fee is their main or even only reliable source of income. Their families have long since lost their patrimony but the title remains. The Lords has thus become a system of outdoor relief for the ex-landed nobility. They pocket their dole in exactly the same spirit of listless self-righteousness with which unmarried teenage mothers collect their social security. Such noblemen are to be seen daily, when Parliament is sitting, escorting their wives and daughters to tables in the peers' dining room – possibly with the hope of picking up husbands for them among lords slightly less indigent than themselves – or entertaining opulent guests, usually described as 'company directors' or 'business executives', in the hope of earning an honest penny. Not having much cash, even for tips – especially for tips, I am sorry to say – they are given short shrift by the servants who treat them with exactly the same combination of nominal servility and genuine contempt that senior NCOs reserve for gentleman-cadets at Officer Training Schools. Elderly viscounts have their toes trodden on and decrepit earls are sent sprawling by beefy waitresses carrying loaded trays. '*Do* you mind, my Lord?' Or 'I beg your Lordship's pardon but if your Lordship *will* get in the way what does your Lordship expect?' There is an air of seedy mendicancy about the place, belied by its magnificent décor, so that the visitor feels thankful to escape without being buttonholed by some leathery old dodger anxious to cash a cheque or borrow a fiver to 'tide him over'. (In fact this is unlikely to happen, as even the most impecunious peers can get credit from Parliament itself and some, I am told, have not paid their dining and bar bills for over a year.)

The large number of hereditary English peers who use the Lords' facilities causes such problems of overcrowding that the inquirer is tempted to ask why the number of such peers is not limited too, and a manageable quota elected, as with Scotland and Ireland. The answer is that the notion of 'representative peers' followed from the closing down of the Edinburgh parliament by the Act of Union 1707 and of the Dublin parliament following the Act of Union of 1800. The English parliament, or rather the English House of Lords, was not prepared to take in an unlimited number of barefoot gallow-glass thanes or a gallimaufry of titled squireens from the bogs of Connaught. Does that mean, then, that the Celts as a group count for less in Parliament than the English? Certainly not. Or that Scottish and Irish nobles as individuals don't carry quite the same weight in the lobbies as English ones? Well, not exactly. But it is best not to dig too deeply into such arcane matters. There are many rules and proceedings connected with the House of Lords which defy rational explanation. It is less a democratic, more a quasi-religious institution, and at its heart is a mystery, or rather a series of mysteries.

One mystery is precisely the Lords Spiritual, who symbolise the religious element. These lords were originally individual members of Parliament because they were tenants-in-chief by knight-service. The sixty or so abbots and priors who also attended on a similar basis were eliminated by Henry VIII in the 1530s when he seized their estates for the Crown, decapitating two abbots in the process. The bishops remained because they kept their estates, or most of them. Now these estates, in turn, have been swallowed up by the Church Commissioners, and the bishops are paid modest salaries. So why are they in the House of Lords? Because, presumably, they are bishops. But not all bishops sit in the Lords, any more than all Irish or Scottish peers do. Indeed, some bishops are more equal than others. The Archbishops of Canterbury and York sit there as of right, simply because they are archbishops. But so also do the bishops of London, Durham and Winchester. This privilege of the Bishop of London might be defended, I suppose, on the grounds that London is the most populous, and difficult, see in the country. But Durham is there simply because, in the Middle Ages, the bishop was also a Count Palatine, with quasi-sovereign powers. The only relic of this today is his round seal (as opposed to an oval one), the badge of royalty. Otherwise he is an ordinary bishop and the see is not even popular among the Anglican *papabile*: it was turned down as cold and inconvenient by several clergymen (or their wives) before the prattlesome David Jenkins got it in 1984. Winchester is similarly privileged entirely because, in the Middle Ages, it was the richest see in England. But it has long since been carved up and its bishop put on salary like the rest. Many bishops are not in the Lords at all. Why? Because the number of other bishops who sit there is limited to twenty-one. Why this particular number? No explanation. And do these twenty-one sit there because they are elected, as 'representative bishops', by their brethren? No. They sit there by seniority of appointment irrespective of the size and importance of their sees. What is the rationale of this system and why does it differ from the one used by Scottish and Irish temporal peers? No explanation.

A further mystery arises when we enquire why only Anglican bishops sit in the House of Lords. Is this because the Church of England is the church of the great majority of the British people? No. Most English people could probably be described as agnostics. They certainly do not go to church. Is the Church of England then the largest Christian church in England? No. The Catholic Church has the most communicants by far, and after that come the nonconformist churches. Why, then, do twenty-six Anglican bishops sit in the Lords? Because they are leaders of the state church, by law established, under the Act of 1559. Does this mean, then, that non-Anglican religious leaders may not sit in the Lords? No. The Methodist leader, Lord Soper, sits there. So does the former Chief Rabbi, Lord Jacobovits. Is this because of the numbers of the Methodists and Jews? No. It is because Prime Minister Harold Wilson admired Lord Soper's left-wing views on secular matters, and because Prime Minister Margaret Thatcher admired Lord Jacobovits's right-wing views on secular matters. Are the Catholics, as the largest Christian community in England, represented by bishops in the Lords? No. Why? No explanation.

A further mystery is provided by the actual conduct of the Anglican bishops in the Lords. Most of them are assiduous attenders. This may be partly because they need the attendance money to supplement their exiguous stipends. But is it not also because they are anxious to defend Christian beliefs and interests in a secular age when they are coming under increasing attack? Not at all. There is indeed an informal pro-Christian lobby in the Lords, but the bishops do not belong to it. The only occasion when they voted in unison in recent years was in trying to resist Sunday opening for shops. This was a straightforward trade union issue, as it were, when the professional interests of clergy were under threat from commerce, and the bishops stuck together. As a rule, however, the bishops cannot be relied upon to defend Christianity with their votes. Quite the contrary. If the content of religious teaching in the schools is put to the vote, most bishops always put ecumenism before Christianity. As a secular peer who belongs to the Christian lobby put it to me: 'When a contentious issue involving Christianity comes up, I regard the bench of bishops as dodgy. Some are far more likely to vote against us than with us. But usually they get hopelessly confused and end by dividing right down the middle.' What the bishops assuredly are not is representative. Their speeches and votes do not reflect the views of ordinary Christians or even of ordinary Anglicans. It is hard to say what they reflect. The bishops differ widely in their religious beliefs. Some do not appear to accept the basic tenets of Christianity or even to believe in God. If the bench of bishops were abolished tomorrow, it is hard to believe that the spiritual content of the House of Lords would be much diminished.

But at least the Lords Spiritual are not corrupt. No case of simony involving a bishop has been recorded in England for centuries. When we come to the life peers, the third main element in the House of Lords, a different situation arises. (Hereditary peers are now created only in exceptional circumstances and need not concern us.) Life peers are created by the Queen but on the recommendation of the Prime Minister alone.

It is probably the single most important element in his personal patronage and is highly valued by Prime Ministers, Labour as well as Conservative. Indeed it is probably more valued by Labour than by Conservative premiers, as one means of keeping order in the ranks of their followers. Now that peers are paid to attend, securing a peerage brings not merely the delights of a title and the comforts of a magnificent free club but a substantial pension for life. This is a point of real substance for the great majority of Labour politicians, who have no private income to rely on when they retire. The Prime Minister's ability to embellish and enrich their declining years is one reason why Labour Cabinet ministers find it convenient to support him in difficult times. Indeed the hope of a peerage, however distant (as opposed to a mere knighthood, which carries no stipend and anyway is not the form on the Labour side), is something a Labour premier can dangle in front of his backbenchers too. Even on the Tory side, the value to the Prime Minister of his right to create peers is rising, as more and more Tory MPs are professional politicans with no substantial outside financial interests. As for the leader of the Liberal Democrats, his right to nominate a small annual quota of life peers is the only substantial piece of patronage he has, and is valued accordingly.

In short, the leaders of all three parties have a strong vested interest in keeping the Lords going as a system of patronage. That is why it remains unreformed. Labour threatens changes or even abolition from time to time, and proposals are set down in its electoral manifestos. But Labour has formed governments in 1924, 1929, 1945, 1964 and 1974. None has carried through Parliament a democratic reform of the Lords, or seriously tried to. When it comes to the point, a Labour Prime Minister always puts his patronage before the people. Indeed, the one systematic attempt to reform the Lords since the war, the Parliament Number Two Bill of 1969, would merely have strengthened the patronage element of the Prime Minister (and of the Leader of the Opposition), without making the second chamber in the smallest degree democratic. That is why Michael Foot MP and Enoch Powell MP combined together to destroy it.

The life-peerage system, then, is an important element in patronage and thus in political corruption. But there is more to it than that. It is arguable that it involves financial corruption too. All systems of honours leave themselves open to abuse. James I, for instance, invented baronetcies or hereditary knighthoods precisely so that he could sell them. When the honours system passed into the hands of the government, which it did increasingly in the eighteenth century and almost wholly in the nineteenth, it was used mainly to keep up majorities in the Commons – that was why William Pitt the Younger debauched the peerage by honouring men who controlled or bought parliamentary boroughs. But with the extension of the suffrage in the second half of the nineteenth century, and the consequent need to create and finance expensive party machines, governments began to use honours for electoral purposes.

The practice began on a large scale during the long prime-ministerships of Lord Salisbury in the last two decades of the nineteenth century. The Chief Whip, or the Patronage Secretary to give him his formal title, and the Chairman of the Conservative Party (or its Treasurer) were the men who directed this system; the Prime Minister, as a rule, preferred to keep his hands clean. The Liberals followed the Conservatives' bad example when they got the chance. By the time of the First World War, the two big parties were, to a great extent, being financed by the sale of honours. The scandal came to a head under the Lloyd George post-war coalition because Lloyd George, not controlling a party, sold honours wholesale in order to build up a party fund of his own with which to finance candidates. He succeeded, and the 'Lloyd George Fund', entirely created by the sale of titles, mainly knighthoods, remained a factor in British politics until Lloyd George gave up his ambitions and went into the House of Lords himself. His abuses were one reason why his coalition collapsed at the end of 1922, and as a result a body of senior statesmen known as the Political Honours Scrutiny Committee was set up. It vets names before they are forwarded to the Queen for her approval, and it functions to this day.

Whether it functions effectively is a matter of argument. Its work is shrouded in secrecy and it cannot be considered a democratic device in any sense of the word. It is a clubman's safety net to keep out 'undesirables', and it does succeed in catching the odd fishy candidate. What it has not done, however, is to eliminate the financial element from the honours system. There is a real problem here, though it is seldom openly discussed in Britain. Democratic political campaigning is hideously expensive and getting more so. In the United States, where running for office is highly individualistic, candidates have to amass their own funds, thus inviting corruption of all kinds. In the last twenty years Congress has passed elaborate laws to eliminate abuses, with mixed results. Some European countries try to get round the problem by providing party funds from the taxpayer, money being handed over in accordance with the number of registered party members or seats held. But many regard this device as highly undesirable because by perpetuating the status quo it afflicts the political system with arteriosclerosis, an undemocratic condition to which it is liable anyway. Nor does it stop abuses. In fact, corruption created by the needs of political parties for electoral finance is now the greatest single evil in Continental politics. It is to be found virtually everywhere but is particularly flagrant in France, Spain and, above all, Italy. Continental governments do not have honours to sell but they have something even more valued, contracts. This form of political corruption is believed to have cost the Italian people over $20 billion in the last fifteen years and has now led to nationwide upheaval.

    In Britain, the sums involved in keeping party machines going are comparatively modest and are largely supplied openly. The Labour Party's financing by the trade unions through the political levy is a form of corruption, as I have already explained, but at least everyone knows about it and some efforts are being made to phase it out. The Conservative Party's financing by business is much more shadowy. The party still refuses to publish details of who gives what. But public companies are obliged to provide figures of contribu-tions under the Companies Act, and by assiduous combing through company accounts the Labour Research Department strips bare some of the Conservative Party's financial underpinning. But many private companies also contribute and so, too, do rich businessmen as individuals, and these figures are not normally available. The fact is that Conservative Prime Ministers do give large numbers of knighthoods and even peerages to business leaders, and a high proportion of them are connected to firms which also make large contributions to Conservative Party funds. Despite all the denials by governments, the Scrutiny Committee and others – Lord Goodman in 1993 wrote a delightful letter to *The Times* saying that 'as one who has had a great deal to do with the award of honours' he could assure everyone that the system was free from corruption – there is clearly a connection between money paid and honours received. Of course, a company chairman in search of a knighthood, and still more of a peerage, will be careful to contribute from his own pockets to popular charities and to form close associations with one or more of them: that is the official high road to the higher honours, and such gifts can always be cited as the reason why peerages are bestowed. But the really substantial sums of cash come from company funds and go straight to Conservative Central Office. Thus the real difference between the old system and the new is that in Lloyd George's day rich men bought peerages directly with their own money; now they buy them indirectly with their shareholders' money.

Such peerages, happily, remain ornamental. They are for show. Rich businessmen do not buy their way into the House of Lords with their company's contributions in order to exert political power. They can do that more effectively in other ways. I am referring now to Conservative businessmen. There are, it is true, a much smaller number of Labour businessmen who have bought their way into the Lords during socialist terms of office. They, being ideologues of a sort, are much more likely to show up, vote and even make speeches. Indeed, one or two have made pestilential nuisances of themselves in the Upper House. That is certainly what would have happened if the late Robert Maxwell had become a life peer, and we can be sure that, if he had lived and contrived to stay afloat, he would indeed have ended up in the Lords. But Tory businessmen-peers do not as a rule contribute to the overcrowding of the

Lords' facilities or exploit their ill-gotten membership of
Parliament.

The most assiduous of all attenders are the Labour life peers,
the great majority of them former members of Labour governments, trade union leaders and the like. These old men (and a
few women) throng the Lords when Parliament is sitting partly
because they have absolutely nothing else to do, partly because
they are heavily dependent on their attendance money and
partly also because they have an incurable itch for public
mischief-making or, as they would put it, discharging their
responsibilities to the nation. The existence of this large and
slowly growing block of Labour peers and peeresses, who are
always there, always vote and often take a detailed part in the
business of the Lords, explains why, despite the existence of a
large, built-in theoretical majority of hereditary peers, the
Conservatives are often hard put to secure a majority in the
Lords and their governments are, from time to time, beaten
there.

Not that Labour life peers spend their time entirely on
making mischief for the nation. A minority are operators on
their own account. The kind of businessman who finds it
convenient to profess socialism and buy himself a Labour life
peerage is not one to neglect to exploit his title and status for
financial purposes. The fact is that Labour Prime Ministers
have sent a number of disreputable people to the Lords, at least
one of whom has actually gone to gaol. The late Lord Bradwell,
or Tom Driberg MP as he was more commonly known, the
most unsavoury man to sit in the Lords this century, was
used by both the Soviet and the British secret services, and
was in addition a well-known 'cottager'. He failed to get into
trouble while a member of the House of Lords entirely because
he received his peerage only nine months before he died, when
he was already ill and, besides, busy writing his scatological
memoirs. Oddly enough, one of the few iniquitous things
Driberg/Bradwell did not do was work for the late Robert
Maxwell. But no less than a score of other life peers did, some in
quite senior positions in the Maxwell organisation. One or two
of them, at least, must have been privy to the dubious nature of
his enterprises, and all of them knew they were treading on thin

ice. The existence of so many life peers in Maxwell's employ, most of them appointed entirely because of the spurious respectability conferred by their titles, is living proof that the Political Honours Scrutiny Committee has not succeeded in cleansing the system (as indeed was the elevation of Lord Bradwell, whose notorious private character must have been well-known to its members; but of course Driberg/Bradwell did not pay for his peerage, as he was perennially in debt).

Life peers of all three parties constitute the biggest single group from which appointments to senior quangos are made. During the last Labour governments of Lords Wilson and Callaghan, Labour life peers got the lion's share of the feast the quangos provide, especially of the well-paid jobs. Now the goodies are more evenly distributed between the parties. One SDP life peer, for instance, earns £42,500 a year as deputy chairman of the Police Complaints Authority. A former Labour minister, now a peer, is both deputy chairman of the London Docklands Development Corporation and vice-chairman of the BBC, bringing him in a total of £38,000 a year. But a group of Conservative life peers, according to a survey made by the *Observer*, hold quango jobs worth a total of £650,000 a year, and one of them, on £92,000 a year, is paid more than the Prime Minister.

The holding of quango jobs ties the life peers into the non-democratic system of self-appointed and non-elected power centres. It has sometimes been argued, by defenders of the House of Lords, that its members are more in touch with ordinary people, and popular sentiment, than MPs. That is a myth. It may be that some of the hereditary peers speak for widespread country sentiments on such issues as rural sports. But they rarely attend and never take part in the inner life of the Lords. On all the principal subjects where the House of Commons has shown itself unrepresentative of public opinion – on crime and punishment, education, welfare spending, permissive sex and public subsidy of culture, for example – the House of Lords, by its votes, has shown itself still more so. The core of the Lords, those who attend regularly, speak often and sit on its committees, who take an active part in piloting legislation through or tabling amendments to Commons bills, can be accurately described as the older generation of the chattering classes. Such men and women are natural members of lobbies, pressure groups and 'communities'. They may wield little direct power as peers, but their influence on public life is considerable and their membership of quangos and other bodies reinforces their ability to exert pressure on ministers and civil servants. They are, all in all, an important part of the ruling establishment and a profoundly undemocratic one.

In 1993, the House of Lords was given, as it happens, a splendid opportunity to show that, though privileged and non-elected, it could still speak for the nation. After the Maastricht Treaty had dragged itself through the Commons, usually by wafer-thin majorities or even none at all, and after the government had finally made it clear that under no circum-stances would it permit a referendum, the Lords had a chance to demonstrate its independence, its populism and its ability to represent those who had been stripped of their democratic rights by ministers. With the polls showing clearly that a majority of the electorate opposed the Maastricht Treaty, and that still more wanted the chance to vote on the issue, like the French, Danes and Irish, the Lords could have voted against the government and forced it to think again. Some opponents of Maastricht fondly and foolishly thought it would do so. But in the largest turnout of peers it has ever contrived, peers of all kinds, Labour, Conservative, Liberal-Democrat, independent, hereditary peers, representative peers, life peers (one aged ninety-five), bishops – the lot – voted overwhelmingly against the popular will and approved the Maastricht Treaty by a majority of close on 250. Thus the last entirely non-elective parliamentary body on earth gave the ordinary people of Britain a contemptuous two-fingered salute.

However, all may not be well in this citadel of privilege. Changes may be coming faster than the peers, enjoying a comfortable lifestyle at the public's expense, seem to think. But that will depend on other factors, and in particular on how other parts of the constitutional scaffolding of this country hold up. At present, some of them appear increasingly shaky. Let us look first at the monarchy.

CHAPTER EIGHT

How the Windsors Failed
to Play Happy Families

*F*rom the 1840s until the end of the 1970s the monarchy was one of the central pillars of British social stability. It was also, paradoxically, a powerful democratic force, for in many respects it reflected the views and upheld the standards of the great majority of ordinary people. It bred popular content because it persuaded British men and women of all classes that at the summit of their society was a reigning family which, despite its wealth and privilege, were like themselves in the things that really mattered – patriotism, principles, morals, domesticity, tastes, love of sport and contempt for intellectual pretentiousness.

It was not always thus. As recently as the 1820s, the dreadful sons of George III, himself a much-loved monarch, threatened to turn Britain into a republic with their profligacy, extravagance and disgusting behaviour. 'Between them,' complained the Duke of Wellington, 'they have insulted every gentleman in the kingdom.' And, he might have added, made passes at most of the ladies. The eldest, the future George IV, was drunk on his wedding night, parted with his wife soon after and attempted – and failed – to get rid of her in a sensational case in the House of Lords which kept the entire country in uproar for six months. His brothers burdened the taxpayers with innumerable mistresses, bastards and debts. Only one produced a legitimate offspring, the Princess Victoria.

However, Victoria not only saved her line but inaugurated a

golden age of British monarchy. She made herself respected, and ultimately deeply loved – not only in Britain but throughout her enormous empire – because she was a decent, ordinary woman, hardworking and dutiful, with a passionate devotion to her family, a simple love of country and a strong belief in God and the Ten Commandments. She may have 'strengthened' her claret with whisky, as Gladstone noted, and permitted harmless liberties to her Highland servant, but her public conduct was always above reproach and on most of the great issues of the day she spoke with the simple, firm, authentic tones of the British people.

The monarchy, thus re-established in popular favour, flourished mightily. King Edward VII happily did not come to the throne until he was in his sixties and had learned discretion. The intelligentsia did not like him but the public, like his sensible wife, Queen Alexandra, turned a blind eye to his elderly liaisons with discreet society women; he was a popular figure yachting, racing, shooting and eating. On political and international matters he was always sensible and often wise. His son, George V, was a model constitutional monarch. The historian G. M. Young once wrote: 'The danger of an educated king is that he would be bound to find some section of his subjects ridiculous.' No such risk in George V's case. His ambitions did not soar beyond his stamp collection and his shoots. He bullied his children but otherwise led an exemplary family life. He was a country gent whose tastes were lower-middle-class and who preferred the workers to the aristocracy. He got on famously with the new breed of Labour Cabinet minister, he lived through the General Strike and the Great Depression without once being accused of taking sides, and his Silver Jubilee, in 1935, produced an outbreak of popular fervour which astonished him: 'I really think they like me for myself,' he noted, pleased but puzzled.

Where George V was modest, his eldest son, Edward VIII, was vain. He was also frivolous, superficial, pleasure-seeking, selfish and irresponsible; and when he determined to marry a twice-divorced American woman he was quickly hustled off the stage into exile. His subsequent behaviour underlined how wise it was to dispose of his services. His brother, George VI, resembled their father in his sense of duty, ordinary views, love of family and simple patriotism. As a bonus, he brought up his two daughters with affectionate warmth. Perhaps because of this, his eldest daughter, who succeeded him as Queen Elizabeth II in 1952, has followed closely in his constitutional footsteps for more than forty years. She has made the occasional mistake, usually because she received bad advice from her Prime Minister of the day. She is shy and limited, does not find it easy to smile (like Queen Victoria) and is sometimes depicted as chilly. It may be, indeed, that she is more fully at home with horses and dogs than with people. But that applies to many of her subjects, and even to the remainder the preference is unobjectionable. The ordinariness of the Queen is her great strength. So is her virtue, consistency, neatness, fortitude and palpable content when surrounded by her family. The British do not love her in the way they love her mother but they find her reassuring. As her reign continues, she becomes increasingly, as Sherlock Holmes said of Dr Watson, 'the one fixed point in a changing world'.

But a change has come over the British royal family in the past two decades, and the Queen has proved powerless to prevent it. There is a widespread feeling, not so much among the ordinary people of the country as among those who wish to influence them – the opinion-formers – that 'in a democratic age' (as they put it), the royal family should be 'more like the rest of us'. That is a foolish error and can only be made by those who have not thought deeply or who do not care sincerely about the institution of monarchy. The best way in which a monarch can attune to an era of democracy is by performing his or her constitutional duties well, by upholding the highest standards of probity and by reflecting the views of the right-thinking majority. That is what Queen Victoria did and it is what George V and George VI did. It is what Queen Elizabeth II has earnestly tried to do.

There is no evidence whatever that most people want a monarch to live like themselves. Quite the reverse. They expect the Queen to wear a crown on appropriate occasions, they want her to be resplendent in glittering jewels at a court ball, they enjoy the spectacle when, in full uniform, she reviews the guards Trooping the Colour. If they are lucky enough to get an invitation to a royal garden party, they like it to be a grand and formal occasion. When the Queen visits their district, they look forward to seeing her arrive in a gleaming Rolls-Royce, surrounded by important personages led by the Lord Lieutenant. They think it right that the Queen should voyage abroad in her yacht, *Britannia*, or use an aircraft of the Royal Flight. They do not envy her her palaces and country homes, her wealth, her servants, her magnificent collection of paintings or any other of the trappings of sovereignty. They consider them all to be part of the national heritage, the warp and woof of an ancient and honourable history of which they are proud. They feel they share in all these things simply by being British citizens, subjects of the Crown and heirs to a great nation. What belongs to the Queen by right and inheritance is hers and they want her to have it, knowing that it is also, in a real sense, theirs too. In short, they want the royal soap opera, as Malcolm Muggeridge called it, to continue.

It was not, then, the people but the opinion-formers who started to rewrite the script. They liked the idea of the royals moving out of their Alice-in-Wonderland existence, stepping through the looking glass, and joining 'the people'. They argued that the younger royals should be freed of the 'stuffy trappings' of 'outmoded protocol', should be allowed to 'live their own lives' and make decisions without 'restrictions imposed by court flunkeys from an earlier era'. In particular, they insisted that young princes and princesses should be allowed to marry whom they chose, and not those whom their parents and advisers thought suitable.

It is at this point that the opinion-formers showed their lack of historical understanding. Royalty is a show. It had always been a show. It must be a show because it has little to do with logic or reason or utility. It is there to delight, to impress, to hold in awe and to edify. It is part theatre, part religious service. The performers or celebrants need to be separated from the audience/congregation. The show doesn't work if the actors leave the stage and start chatting to people in the stalls, or if those who come to worship are encouraged to invade the high altar. And in order to preserve these all-important distinctions, all kinds of conventions are needed – protocol, bowing, 'Ma'am-ing' and 'Sir-ing', men in uniforms, footmen in knee-breeches, titles, orders and other baubles, foolish in themselves perhaps but markers and trip-wires, performing the same function as greasepaint and footlights on the stage, or vestments and incense at the altar.

Naturally, the markers, trip-wires – or taboos, if you like – are, or at any rate were, most formidable in the zone of marriage. In the past, royal marriages were affairs of state, important diplomatic events. Two royal families joined in matrimony to bring peace or alliance or mutual advantage to their nations. They also preserved the blood royal. These considerations count for much less today, but there is one respect in which the case for royals marrying royals is as strong as ever: codes of conduct. Royals are not like the rest of us. They are required to perform on stage, to officiate at sacred ceremonies. We are the onlookers. Their trade is full of professional secrets, tricks and mysteries, best acquired by those brought up to it from birth. It is a hereditary profession, and for good reason. So the best royal marriages are indeed dynastic.

Being royal is not about wealth. It is not even about landed property. It is about birth and conduct. The line of distinction runs between royals and the rest of us. For this purpose, dukes and earls, viscounts and barons stand with the *hoi polloi* outside the royal enclosure. This may strike most people as odd but there are good reasons for it. Royalty is royal, or it is nothing. There is in Germany a kind of reservoir of royalty, two or three score of families which were once the sovereign rulers of kingdoms and archduchies or palatinates. Many of them are far from wealthy. Their homes, though called palaces, are austere and often ill-heated. Their formal clothes may be grand but are sometimes inherited, like their quarterings. What marks them out from the rest of us is their upbringing. They feel themselves to be – they are – members of a caste. They were born to be royals and nothing else. Some of course have professions. But their work is secondary to their royalness. They are trained to be naval or army officers, sometimes diplomats. But their real function is to marry other royals, and beget yet more royals in their turn.

Such people have their uses on the giant chessboard of Europe. In the second half of the nineteenth century they supplied new royal lines for the Balkan kingdoms liberated from the Turks. And, in a royal marriage market not over-provided with choice, they turned out princes and princesses available for matrimony. Queen Victoria selected a handsome member of the caste for her husband. So did Queen Elizabeth II. Edward VII was fortunate to secure a daughter of a reigning house. George V took his bride from the German reservoir. George VI married when he had no prospect of becoming king, choosing a Scottish lady he loved and whom he had pursued doggedly for two years. She adapted to her role with aplomb and in time became *plus royaliste que le roi*, leading the palace guard dogs in keeping the wretched Duchess of Windsor outside the enclosure.

As a rule, the British royal family stuck to the caste and had no reason to regret it. A prince or princess may be penniless but if he or she is brought up to the rules of the caste a royal marriage is no problem. And the rules are complex only in the details; the central command is simplicity itself. It is: Never let down the royal side. The demands of the sovereign trade union comes first. Or, to put it another way, the show of monarchy must go on. A princess may be married to a sovereign who is a drunkard or an adulterer – or both – or a homosexual or transvestite or a bore, a bigot, a bully or a monster in human shape. But she carries on regardless, observing the proprieties, keeping her dignity, producing children and showing her husband all the marks of external respect. Divorce or desertion is out of the question. At all costs, appearances must be kept up. The princess is taught this from birth. She is told that God put her on earth not to be happy, but to be royal. And in her own way, by doing her duty under difficulties, she *is* happy, too.

Such princesses, and their male equivalents, kept the international royal soap opera on the road. They continue to be available in our own times. There has never been any shortage of German royals. But of course they are not necessarily eye-catching. They are built for use and durability, for the long matrimonial haul, not for delight. Hence by the 1950s or thereabouts, princes of reigning houses were beginning to look around for themselves. The opinion-formers, the modernisers, were encouraging them to do so. Princess Margaret was the first to break ranks. Her eye fell on a handsome courtier, a war hero but a commoner. Alas, he was divorced. So he would not do and the princess herself came to see it in that light. She said to Archbishop Fisher, who came to admonish her armed with his references, 'You may put away your books, Archbishop, I do not intend to marry Group Captain Townsend.' So that was that. But when the princess's eye then fell on a photographer, Anthony Armstrong-Jones, no one had the steely resolution to break her heart again. So she married him and he was made an earl; they had children and in due course they were divorced.

Thus the spell of royal rectitude was broken. Of course Princess Margaret was no longer in the direct line of succession to the throne, so perhaps her breaking of the divorce taboo was not considered critical. But it did indicate that royals were beginning to behave like rich, titled members of the international jet set and treat marriage as an exercise in pleasure-seeking, to be abandoned when convenient, rather than a sanctified contract for life. And it set a precedent. The opinion was now formed that royal offspring, however close to the throne, might look around for themselves and marry whom they fancied, rather than observe royal house rules. So in due course three out of four of the Queen's children, including the heir to the throne, married commoners: an army officer, the daughter of an earl, the daughter of a polo manager. Children were born and in due course these three marriages too ended in breakdown.

All this was tragic for those concerned, awkward and obviously distressing for the Queen. But it might not have damaged the monarchy but for another factor – the growing intrusiveness and impudence of the media. The English monarchy's relationship with the scribes has been uneven over the centuries. Some medieval kings fell foul of contemporary monastic chroniclers – William II ('Rufus') and King John ('Lackland') were particularly roughly handled and their reputations have never since recovered. In the case of Edward II, another victim of the contemporary media, we are even treated to details of the horrible manner in which he was murdered as John Trevisa, a sort of fourteenth-century gossip-writer, tells us it was 'with a hoote broche putte thro the secret place posterialle'. In the Georgian era royal miscreants, especially George III's gruesome sons, suffered severely at the hands of the producers of satirical prints: for instance, over 500 different ones, many of them obscene, survive depicting George IV's abortive attempt to convict his wife of adultery. The scabrous details of this trial, which lasted many weeks, were reported verbatim in the newspapers, now mass-printed on the new steam presses: William Wilberforce MP describes buying no fewer than twelve of them on Sunday and devouring their coverage of the trial 'with ever-increasing disgust'. The English had already discovered the humbugging delights of deploring the salacity of the press while buying more and more news-papers. But in those days journalists played a risky game. The authorities, if so minded, could use the law of criminal libel, against which truth was not in itself a defence, against penny-a-liners who brought royalty into ridicule or contempt. George IV, while still Prince Regent, had the satisfaction of seeing the poet Leigh Hunt, who was also editor of the *Examiner*, gaoled for two years and fined £500 (about £75,000 in our money) in 1813 for a 'foul, atrocious and malignant libel' on the heir to the throne. Charles Lamb, who actually wrote the piece, was lucky to escape undetected.

With Victoria, and the beginnings of modern decorous monarchy, the press signed an unofficial ceasefire, which continued almost to our own day. When Edward, Prince of Wales, later Edward VII, got himself into the witness box as a result of his fondness for gambling – this happened in the 'Tranby Croft affair' (1891) – or for society ladies – the Mordaunt divorce case (1870) – the more scurrilous papers treated him as fair game. But they left his mistresses alone and they certainly did not dog his footsteps when, for instance, he visited his favourite Paris brothels, one of which had an imitation railway compartment fitted to serve his propensities. Edward VIII, when Prince of Wales, enjoyed being treated as a celebrity by the press – he was the first modern hero of the *paparazzi* – but had a code of signals to photographers to indicate when he wished to remain anonymous. This was honoured, as was the taboo on any mention of his affair with the divorced Mrs Simpson, right to the eve of his abdication. It is worth remembering indeed that the public silence on the king's behaviour in 1936 was broken not by the media but by an Anglican bishop, perhaps inadvertently.

Throughout the reign of George VI, and for many years into the reign of his daughter, the media treated royalty with unalloyed adulation. By the second half of the 1950s, the extent of royal coverage had become so monumental, and the tone so cloying, as to invite a reaction. I remember well when it happened. One morning in 1957 Kingsley Martin came into my office at the *New Statesman* and slapped down on my desk an article he had just been sent by Malcolm Muggeridge: 'Read that. It's a crackerjack [his favourite term of praise]. The best article I have ever read.' This was the famous 'Royal Soap Opera', which first broke the taboo on criticising royalty. Re-read today, its tone seems excessively mild, even deferential. Nevertheless, Muggeridge did not escape retribution. When a similar piece appeared in America and aroused transAtlantic controversy, he was banned from the BBC for a time and forced to resign from the Garrick Club.

Even so, the taboo was never quite reimposed. When the 1960s, that meretricious and destructive decade, introduced the habit of attacking all forms of authority just for the hell of it, monarchy came in for its share. Once again, as in 1790–1830, it became not just permissible, but fashionable, to caricature and satirise royalty. Then in time, the doings of royalty began to be reported not just on official occasions but on private ones, not just when it was convenient for them but when it was titillating for readers. In his article Muggeridge had urged Buckingham Palace to set up a proper press machine run by a professional who knew how to handle the media – to master the press by inviting it in, and managing it. That advice was ultimately taken. At the time it seemed wise. In retrospect, I believe it was foolish. The royal family, even the Queen, cooperated with television producers in permitting filming within the sacred palatial precincts. Even interviews were sanctioned, the questions becoming ever more familiar. Editors were invited to lunch. Journalists were recognised, even greeted by their

Christian names. Privileged authors of books on royalty were given facilities and supplied with information 'off the record', sometimes even on it. All this was a risky game, and the royal minders proved to be no good at all. Providing the media with controlled opportunities to cover royalty, far from containing the problem, merely whetted an appetite for uncontrolled ones. During the 1970s and still more in the 1980s, cooperation between the Palace and the media, especially the tabloids, broke down.

The damage could have been limited had the media operated within a sensible legal code. I now very much regret that, when I was a member of the Royal Commission on the Press, 1975-7, I did not urge my colleagues to recommend a privacy law. I believe I could have persuaded them and that, had such a recommendation been made, such a law would have been enacted by the then Labour government, and much future trouble avoided. But I did not then foresee, nor did anyone else, the horrific invasions of privacy, not least royal privacy, which were to take place in the 1980s and still more in the 1990s.

It is true that everyone, including royalty, is protected by the civil law of libel (criminal libel is not much use now). But in civil libel, truth is an absolute defence and plaintiffs can be minutely cross-examined on their actions, views and principles. Evidence thus given is on the public record and publication of it privileged, so it can be printed in full with complete impunity. That was vividly illustrated early in 1994 when an actress from *EastEnders*, suing the *Sun* for libel, was publicly racked in court by the famous George Carman QC on her supposed habit of giving 'blow-jobs'. Royals are thus in practice deterred from using the remedy of civil libel, even when what is published about them is both defamatory and untrue, because it is not worth their while to risk such torture in the witness box.

The advantage of a privacy law, by contrast, is that by making intrusion or theft of privacy a tort, subject to damages, it merely obliges the plaintiff to prove that the intrusion took place. There is no need for the plaintiff even to appear in court as a rule. Truth is no defence; indeed, as in criminal libel, it might even aggravate the damages. The only proper defence – and it is a very proper one indeed – is public interest. Then it is for the jury, a most suitable body in the circumstances, to decide whether the public interest overrides the intrusion. The public interest point can be made by submissions, and it is most improbable that a judge would allow further violation of privacy by hostile cross-examination of the plaintiff, unless the circumstances were wholly exceptional.

The existence of a privacy law would have saved the royal family, as well as innumerable other people, untold damage and grief over the last few years. Some of us have pressed repeatedly for this necessary reform in the law. I must have written a dozen articles calling for it. For a long time ministers told me that their lawyers said such a statute was impracticable and impossible to frame. To which I replied: 'Get yourself some better lawyers,' adding that various other countries had found no difficulty in framing such a law, or enforcing it either. Of course the real reason was the government's fear of the press, especially since 1990. Needless to say, it hated the press too; but its fear was greater. Then, in the autumn of 1993 the balance changed and hatred temporarily drove out fear. A reference to a forthcoming privacy bill appeared in the Queen's speech – it seemed that the government lawyers had suddenly miraculously discovered a way of framing it. But at the time of writing no such bill has been tabled and it may be that fear of the press has again become the overriding consideration for ministers. It should be added that public opinion, all along, has been overwhelmingly in favour of curbing media invasion of privacy. But, as we have repeatedly seen, public opinion counts for little with today's politicians, compared with powerful interests and pressure groups.

Hence, when the marriages of the Queen's children broke down, one by one, there was nothing to protect the family from an intrusive media. Princess Anne was the most fortunate of the three, for her marriage broke down first, before the media had tasted royal blood and so acquired Dutch courage. She and her former husband behaved sensibly and without acrimony. The collapse of the Duke of York's marriage, followed quickly by the revelation that the Prince of Wales's was also crumbling, introduced an entirely different drama. The two wives, not being born royal, made no effort at all to observe the rules of the monarch's trade union and decided to fight their corners. The Duchess of York, indeed, conducted her own publicity, or rather employed an American friend to do it, and soon enabled the media to cover her in ridicule. The Princess of Wales enabled a journalist, Andrew Morton, to get the material to tell her side of the marriage breakdown, and the resulting book, *Diana: Her True Story*, was the most grievous blow inflicted on the British monarchy since Edward VIII's abdication.

Hence, it is important to grasp that, greatly as the media has aggravated the damage suffered by the royal family, the damage was essentially self-inflicted in the first place. By allowing her children to marry whom they chose and still keep their rights of succession, the Queen made a serious error of judgement. The destructive behaviour of the two women who had not been brought up to the trade was predictable. The media merely seized, with both hands, microphones, tapes, telescopic sights and all, on the opportunities presented to them. The government, as might have been expected, behaved with a bewildered lassitude which masked indecision and cowardice.

The marriage breakdowns, followed by the public emergence of the background to them and the moral character of some of those concerned, shattered the magic show of monarchy at least for a time. The scenery was revealed as lath and plaster, the beauty as mere makeup, the costumes as tawdry. Once, as it were, daylight was let into the theatre, the audiences noticed all kinds of things were wrong and began to ask awkward questions. For some time public criticism had been growing, almost unnoticed, about the sheer size of the royal family, as more and more offspring joined the privileged circle and enjoyed its delights. A public consensus began to form: there were just too many royals, and they were too expensive. Eventually notice was taken, and the number of royals with legal status as such was severely reduced. This obvious abuse should have been ended not when it was compelled by public opinion but before the public became aware of it.

More serious was the discovery that the Queen herself did not pay income tax on her private income. Many of us knew about this. What we did not know – what hardly anyone even in the inner circles of authority knew – was that this was a comparatively recent innovation, going back only to 1937. When Edward VIII abdicated his successor, George VI, undertook to pay him an annual sum by way of compensation for loss of office. In return Neville Chamberlain, first Chancellor of the Exchequer, then Prime Minister during the period in question, undertook to make it up to the new king by remitting taxation on his private means. The arrangement was made privately and does not appear to show up in the documents. Since the Duke of Windsor had long been dead when the matter came to light it is curious that the Queen's financial advisers had not volunteered, on her behalf, to pay tax on her private income from the point when the pension to the Duke lapsed. At all events, nothing was done, and once again the Palace was forced to give way in response to public criticism, rather than anticipate it.

A further abuse came to light only in January 1994, in response to a parliamentary question by the Labour MP Alan Williams. It was then revealed that no fewer than 268 people enjoyed rent-free accommodation in the royal palaces. They include members of the royal family and their relatives and friends, and present and former members of the royal staff. Upkeep of the royal palaces, which has been a public charge since the reign of William IV, cost the taxpayer £21.9 million in 1993. Royal servants are not on the whole well paid, nor are their pensions generous. There can be no reasonable objection to old and valued retainers receiving accommodation at low rents or even free. But an investigation by the *Mail on Sunday* established that some of those thus privileged had perfectly good homes of their own, often sumptuous ones, and were comfortably off or even wealthy. Once again, the practice is hard to justify, and the taxpayer is the loser. At the time of writing, the abuse continues, and even when and if it is ended, the Queen will be seen to be yielding to public criticism rather than making it unnecessary by timely reform.

It is not surprising, therefore, that the conduct of the royal family (rather than the monarchical institution as such) has come under increasing criticism in the early 1990s, often from quarters normally staunch in their loyalty. A survey by

Conservative Central Office of party members and constituency officials revealed a disturbing volume of hostile
comment. Middle-aged or elderly traditionalists, fervent
patriots and warm defenders of established values, who a few
years before would never have uttered a word against either the
principle or the practice of royalty, were now questioning both.
The Queen herself was usually exempt from criticism, but even
she was held partly responsible for some abuses, especially
financial ones. Junior members of the royal family came in for
forthright condemnation. Other surveys and polls indicated
that young people, Labour or Conservative or neither, were still
more sceptical or cynical about royalty.

In this respect a dramatic change has occurred during my
lifetime. In the 1930s all schools positively promoted loyalty to
the throne. Photographs of the king and queen hung in
classrooms and assembly halls. The Union Jack was flown and
the National Anthem sung regularly. Schoolchildren played
particularly prominent roles in such celebrations as jubilees
and coronations. I remember well, in my first year at school, the
elaborate preparations the nuns made for celebrating King
George V's Silver Jubilee. They included cutting out and
gluing together an elaborate cardboard model of the entire
jubilee procession. Only those infants of exemplary behaviour
were allowed to cut out the horses, footmen and component
parts of the royal coach itself. The privilege of cutting out the
silhouette of the king and queen was awarded, after fierce
competition and jealous scenes, to a little girl who had earned
the title of 'Best Infant'. Today training in loyalty to the throne
plays no part in state schools. Most teachers observe a total
silence on the subject or, if it crops up, show indifference or even
hostility. At teacher training colleges, monarchy is treated as
Politically Incorrect. It is rare indeed in a state school for a
pupil to hear anything said in defence of constitutional
monarchy, or for that matter in favour of parliamentary
democracy either. They are taught, rather, to assert rights and
formulate grievances. And royalty is fast becoming another
grievance.

But despite the many forces working in our society against
the idea of monarchy, and despite the gaping self-inflicted

wounds from which the royal family now suffers, there is a surprisingly strong residuum of affection for the House of Windsor and a still more powerful instinctive feeling in favour of the Crown as part of our system of government. It is sometimes asserted, especially by academics, that ordinary people lack the capacity or education to pronounce on complex constitutional issues. That is nonsense. In the first place, most fundamental constitutional issues are not complex. They are simple and easily grasped. The idea of selecting and sending people to Parliament to carry out popular wishes is straightforward. So is the business of forming a government from among them. The notion of the head of state, standing above the government and symbolising the entire country, not just one party, is slightly more complicated. But it does not raise insuperable difficulties. Moreover, it is more thoroughly understood – and welcomed – when that head of state is not a routine former politician, here today and gone tomorrow, but the head of an actual family, whose history is intertwined with that of the nation, whose ancestors have sat on the throne for hundreds of years, and whose progeny will, God willing, still be there hundreds of years hence. A president is just another kind of politician. A monarch is special, a creature of quasi-religious value, a focus of glitter and glamour. A king or a queen, born to the purple, raised as a prince or princess, crowned in splendour and reigning with sceptre and orb, personalises the concept of constitutional rule far better than an elected person, who has gone through the mud and bickering of a campaign. It is the palm without the dust. A monarchy is perceived, not just by the common people but by all people, including the most sophisticated, to be above the battle, to embody the national ideal, in a way a presidency cannot. Absurd it may sometimes seem, but in a real sense monarchy is a *natural* form of government, a profoundly human way of ruling.

It is so partly because the monarch is not alone. He or she is the head not just of the nation but of a family. A people are all kinds of things, but most of all they are a collection of families. That is how they see themselves. It is reassuring for them to feel that presiding over them is not a solitary individual, but a queen surrounded by her family, a family just like theirs except in its elevation, with births, marriages, deaths, joys and sorrows, successes and failures, the glorified mirror of their own family lives.

The human and family virtues of constitutional monarchy have been so eloquently expounded by Walter Bagehot in Chapter Two of *The British Constitution* that I need not repeat them here. But present circumstances demand I add this. Precisely because the system is intensely personal, and familiar, it makes particular demands on the persons involved in it. The Queen does not need to be clever. God forbid she should be a genius or a prodigy or a paragon! She need not know Latin or Greek or be an expert computer programmer. It will delight people if she is a keen sportswoman, with a spirit of adventure and a keen sense of humour. It is excellent if she appreciates the beauty of the splendid collections she inherits and adds to them with love and knowledge. But none of this is necessary. What is essential is that she be good, and be seen to be good. And by good I mean exhibit the qualities of simple morality and decency her subjects hold dear. They want her, above all, to set an example.

It is here that democracy comes in. Constitutional monarchy is a marriage – and it can be a highly successful marriage – between the hereditary principle and demotic sentiment. Demotic sentiment demands systematic genuflexion to traditional morality. It has been argued recently that the immoral behaviour of certain younger members of the royal family is no worse than is routine among members of their class today – the rich, the titled, the international jet-setters. That may be so. It may even be better. But such comparisons are irrelevant. Divorce in Britain may be the highest in Europe. One in five children born today may be illegitimate. But the most elaborate survey of the sexual habits (and views) ever made of the British people, which questioned over 17,000 people, revealed when it was published in January 1994 that their moral code and even, to a great extent, their practice were remarkably conservative. Chastity and fidelity are highly valued and respected. Marriage for life is seen not just as the ideal but the norm. The love between spouses, and between parents and their children, is regarded as the natural cement of society, and the nuclear family as the hub around which the wheel of society turns. In short, the Judeo-Christian ethic, as symbolised by the Mosaic Decalogue, is still close to the emotional and spiritual heart of Britain.

That being so, the course for monarchy is clear. The Crown needs to be as democratic as any other part of the constitutional machinery. It achieves this not by giving up its palaces or by riding bicycles and waiting at bus stops. There is no demand for that at all: quite the contrary. The Crown responds to democratic demands, and performs its democratic functions, when it becomes the model and standard of good behaviour. The Queen in particular, and all the principal members of the royal family, must conform, at least externally, to the Judeo-Christian norm. Fidelity must be observed; marriage must be for life; the nuclear family must be preserved intact. The monarch must conform to these ideals herself. But she also has the duty to insist that other members of the family observe the proprieties too, or lose their royal status. The recent troubles of the family spring from weakness in enforcing these democratic demands. Human frailty being what it is, no doubt a certain element of humbug will accompany such conformity. But if hypocrisy is the tribute vice pays to virtue, so it is the genuflexion monarchy makes to democracy. The public does not demand virtue as such. It does not seek, as Queen Elizabeth I put it, 'to carve windows into men's souls'. What it demands is propriety. And the royal family has an absolute obligation to display it.

All that is clear enough. And one might expect that, in struggling to preserve the decencies in response to democratic demands, the royal family – the monarch above all – would have the wholehearted encouragement of the established church, of which indeed she is the Supreme Governor. Alas, matters are not so simple as that. Helping the royal family to be good does not come high among the priorities of a church struggling to keep itself, body and soul, above the rising waters of secularism and infidelity.

CHAPTER NINE

Christianity by Law Established
with God Left Out

*T*he modern decline in the fortunes of the Church of England began long before the monarchy's troubles, has been far more precipitous, and begins to look terminal. The story, a sad one, is essentially the same: that of an ancient institution which no longer provides what the people have the right to expect of it, and is therefore increasingly shunned and despised.

The Church of England is more than four centuries old but it has always had the weakness of its origins. It could be said to suffer from two handicaps and one mixed blessing. The first of its handicaps is that it has always been divided and has never been able to unite, in mind and soul, behind a common set of beliefs. When it came into existence, in the thirty years 1530–60, it consisted of two broad strands: the Catholics, who followed the Crown in its breach with Rome but were otherwise in agreement with most of the teachings of the universal church; and the radicals, who looked to Geneva – most of them later became Calvinists – and who wanted root-and-branch reform, including the abolition of episcopacy. Elizabeth I, under her Act of Supremacy And Uniformity 1559, forced both sections into an uneasy coalition under herself as Supreme Governor. But she had a great deal of trouble keeping the coalition together and under the Stuarts it fell apart, leaving a number of nonconformist churches and an Anglican rump. Under the Hanoverians, the rump spawned first the Wesleyans or Methodists and later reorganised itself into three sections: the

Evangelicals or Calvinists, the Broad Church or Erastians, content to go whither the state directed, and the High Church or Anglo-Catholics, many of whom followed Newman and Manning to Rome. This tripartite fracture still exists today.

As a result of this continual fragmentation, the Church of England has never been a national church in the sense that it has never been voluntarily followed by the great mass of the people. The historians are still arguing about whether the Reformation and the breach with Rome was a popular movement or not. The most likely conclusion is that a majority of Londoners were Protestants of one kind or another, but the rest of the country (except for the far south-west) was predominantly Catholic until well into the seventeenth century. Anglicanism became the norm in a large number of rural districts but it gradually lost its hold on London, and in the new industrial areas it was a non-starter: first the non-conformists, then the Catholics, evangelised the urban masses. Anglicanism had never been, in modern times, more than the church of the ruling class, the rural gentry and poor, and (until recently) of the educated middle class.

Thus handicapped by its divisions and by its weak, non-inclusive popular base, the Church of England has been sustained by its legal status as 'the Church by Law Established'. This gave it all the real estate of the old medieval church, which owned one-fifth of England at the beginning of the 1530s, less what had been plundered under Henry VIII and subsequently. The Anglicans kept the cathedrals and the old parish churches, and in the nineteenth century parliamentary grants enabled them to build thousands of new ones. They also kept cathedral and parish lands, which rose greatly in value in the century 1750–1850, enabling clerical incomes to multiply and vast rectories to be built. Even today, the wealth of the church, now administered collectively by the Church Commissioners, makes the Church of England perhaps the best-endowed religious body in the world. Then, too, Anglicanism is the beneficiary of many legal privileges, ranging from its official status in the courts of law, the armed services, the ancient universities and schools and the royal Court, to its seats in Parliament. Until quite recently, it was able to offer comfortable and even distinguished careers to some of the best-educated members of the middle and upper classes. In short it was, and even still is, held erect by a scaffolding of state support.

But this had, and has, its drawbacks. As a state institution, the Church of England and its clergy are governed by a structure of parliamentary statutes, some of great antiquity, which it is powerless to change except through Parliament. Thus the creed of the church is governed by the Thirty-Nine Articles of 1563, many of which reflect the venomous doctrinal disputes of the mid-sixteenth century. Even under the liberalising statute of 1865 all Anglican clergy must affirm that these articles and the *Book of Common Prayer* are 'agreeable to the Word of God' and undertake not to teach in contradiction to them. Since some of the Articles are absurd, and many Anglican clergy, including bishops, manifestly do not agree with all, or in some cases any, of them, the church's ministers are made to seem humbugs, as of course many of them are. The original 1559 *Book of Common Prayer*, as revised in 1662, has also led to endless trouble, but in 1927–8 a determined attempt by the church leadership to update it was defeated in the House of Commons. Subsequent measures, the Prayer Book (Alternative And Other Services) Measure 1965, as amended by the Church Of England (Worship And Doctrine) Measure 1974, by introducing what are called 'alternative services', have plunged the church's ritual and liturgy into complexity and confusion and left many communicants furious. There is now a chasm between those who idolise the form and language of the ancient liturgy and those determined to make services 'relevant' to 'the needs of the modern age'.

Under intense pressure from the Anglican bishops, or some of them, Parliament has shown itself willing to allow the state church some freedom in ordering itself. But this has merely led to more bickering. In 1919 it passed the Church Of England National Assembly (Powers) Act which created a three-tier assembly (bishops, clergy and laity) with authority to prepare church legislation for Parliament's approval. This merely led to the Prayer Book fiasco. In 1969 the structure of self-government was changed by the Synodical Government Measure, which abolished the assembly and replaced it with a twice-yearly General Synod. This freed the Church of England to some extent from parliamentary control but, by creating a sort of pseudo-parliament of its own, raised fresh problems. The more 'progressive' clergy, led by the majority of the bishops, saw the Synod as the means by which Anglicanism could modernise itself and introduce 'relevance', in doctrine, services, organisation and discipline. The traditionalists insisted that the Synod, which represented only the English portion of the universal church, was powerless to change anything of consequence. The Synod thus became the theatre of ever more acrimonious argument.

This might have been less serious if the episcopate had been able to provide strong leadership, or indeed any kind of leadership. But the circumstances in which bishops are made renders this not quite impossible but inherently unlikely. Diocesan bishops are appointed by the Crown on the advice of the Prime Minister. It is true that the Crown, on the death of the old bishop, gives the dean and chapter of the diocesan cathedral a *congé d'élire*, or leave to proceed to an election. But it also nominates whom they are to elect. It is unlawful for them to refuse. This was made unforgettably clear in 1847 when the Prime Minister Lord John Russell on behalf of the Crown nominated Dr Renn Dickson Hampden to be Bishop of Hereford. When the Dean of Hereford wrote to Russell saying he would vote against Hampden, the Prime Minister replied briefly as follows: 'Sir, I have had the honour to receive your letter of the 23rd instant, in which you intimate to me your intention of violating the law.' Hampden was duly elected, the Dean voting as he was bid.

Until recently, then, bishops were chosen entirely by the head of government, and there was something to be said for this system. A Prime Minister, uninfluenced by membership of an ecclesiastical faction, may be a good judge of personal fitness. W. E. Gladstone, though personally inclined to be High Church, took enormous trouble to discover men fit for a mitre and appointed them, bearing in mind the peculiar needs of each see, irrespective of their leanings and strictly on spiritual and intellectual merit. But other Prime Ministers have been less conscientious. On Derby Day 1894, an Old Etonian called George Kennion, who had just returned from Australia where he had been Bishop of Adelaide, was sitting in the Athenaeum Club. A group of friends told him as a joke that colonial bishops returning from duty were always expected to call on the Prime Minister. The present holder of the post was Lord Rosebery, whom Kennion had known at Eton. So Kennion hastened to Downing Street, where he was redirected to Rosebery's palatial town residence, 38 Berkeley Square. There, naturally, he was told that Rosebery was at Epsom, so left his card. In the evening the Prime Minister returned in triumph from the Derby, which had been won by his horse Ladas. A large crowd cheered in the square, while Rosebery drank a glass of champagne. It was at this moment of euphoria that Kennion's card was brought to him. Rosebery was delighted to be reminded of his old school chum. The bishopric of Bath and Wells happening to be vacant, Rosebery promptly bestowed it on Kennion, who held it until his death twenty-eight years later.

Kennion, by pure chance, was a reasonably good bishop. It often happens that Prime Ministers who are unobservant Anglicans, or non-Anglicans or even non-Christians, appoint good bishops, since they take the advice of some furtive official on their staff whose job it is to know which Anglican clergy are up, and which are down. But a Prime Minister guided by dogmatic or even political considerations can make horrible errors. In 1924 the first Labour Prime Minister, Ramsay MacDonald, nominated to the see of Birmingham a bellicose pacifist called Ernest Barnes. From then until his retirement in 1953, he kept the Church of England in a periodic uproar, preaching what were called his 'Gorilla Sermons', in which he insisted men were descended from apes, and getting himself involved in litigation with archbishops, church patrons and clergy as well as prominent industrialists (he had a particular grievance, none knew why, against the cement industry, and was forced to pay various companies large damages in a libel action). His sermons were also the occasions of demonstrations and even fisticuffs.

Bishop Barnes was not the only political appointment to the bench of bishops to bring the church into damaging controversy, and in 1977 an informal agreement was made to allow a fifteen-strong body called the Crown Appointments Commission to submit two names for each episcopal vacancy, from which the Prime Minister selects one. This seems to have made little difference. In 1984 when the bishopric of Durham became vacant, and various eligible people turned it down, Margaret Thatcher was persuaded into appointing to the see, once one of the most important in the country, a talkative academic called David Jenkins, who (it subsequently emerged) was sceptical about many of the central doctrines of Christianity. Shortly after he was consecrated in York Minster, its splendid north transept was burned down in a mysterious fire, which many traditionalists thought an ill omen or even an angry remonstrance from God. Being a man who craved publicity, Jenkins delighted to come out with controversial pronouncements on doctrine, especially at Christmas and Easter, which brought furious public remonstrances from clergy and layfolk alike. Thus he dismissed the Resurrection as 'a conjuring trick with bones', poured scorn on the Virgin Birth and castigated the New Testament accounts of the Nativity as fairy tales. He varied his denials of Christian doctrines with left-wing pronouncements on politics and ill-considered interventions in the House of Lords, where he sat *ex-officio*. As Lord Whitelaw, then Conservative Leader of the House of Lords, observed to me: 'I always hope the Bishop of Durham will come out on their [i.e. Labour's] side. He is sure to swing us votes.'

With foolish men like Barnes and Jenkins liable to bring the established chuch into disrepute, much depended on the wisdom of the Archbishop of Canterbury. On the whole, at least until half-way through the twentieth century, the Anglican primates were well chosen. Most of them appreciated that their job was to keep the coach on the road at all costs, and concentrated on the largely secular task of managing ill-disciplined and egocentric wheel-horses. The job of the Archbishop was not so much to evangelise as to prevent an internal catastrophe by shrewd prodding and persuading and an occasional flick of the disciplinary whip. The last Archbishop to do this with any success was Geoffrey Fisher, Archbishop of Canterbury 1945–61. He had been an outstanding headmaster of Repton, transforming a rebellious school into one of the best in the country by personally flogging large numbers of bad boys. While at Lambeth, his brisk and authoritative style kept the show on the road. But since he retired it has been downhill all the way.

The creation of the synodal system was bound to lead to crisis sooner or later, since the gap between the radicals, who wanted it to 'reform' the church, and the traditionalists, who insisted it had no spiritual power to do so, was unbridgeable. Robert Runcie, Archbishop of Canterbury 1981–91, managed to postpone open breaches on a number of issues, and especially on the desire of the Synod radicals to introduce women priests, by skilful wheeler-dealing. But that led him into endless and unedifying compromises, obfuscations and Janus-faced pronouncements, which avoided war only at the cost of presenting the Church of England as a body which stood for nothing very much, led or rather presided over by shifty and devious men. Nor was Runcie unable to prevent, and perhaps did not wish to do so, the introduction of women deacons into the church. By the early 1990s there were over 1200 of these women ministers, half of them stipendiaries working full-time; one-fifth of all those in Anglican seminaries were women. Since men and women were consecrated deacons at exactly the same time, after undergoing exactly the same training, and since the men were automatically ordained priest after the lapse of a year, and appointed to a benefice after a further year, the discrimination against women on the grounds of sex alone became an open scandal, and was thought to be intolerable in the intellectual climate of the 1990s, where they were being advanced in every other profession including the armed services.

How a man like Fisher would have handled the crisis it is hard to say. But not many could have made so thorough a mess of it as Runcie's successor, Dr George Carey. He was a late recruit to the ministry, a bit of an autodidact, thought to be sensible and 'sound'. He turned out to be a first-class booby and soon succeeded in annoying politicians and churchgoers alike with his ill-considered remarks. His intervention in the women-priests controversy was particularly unfortunate since he kicked off not merely by backing the women – which he was quite entitled to do – but by castigating their opponents as 'heretics'. This was not merely unwise but strictly against Anglican usage, and Carey was forced to retract and apologise. The final Synod debate in 1993 began against a background of recrimination, and when the proposal to ordain women priests was carried by a tiny minority, the high road was opened to schism with up to 2000 Anglican clergy led by the former Bishop of London, Dr Graham Leonard, considering leaving the church and joining Rome, like Cardinals Manning and Newman before them. If such an exodus were to take place – and, at the time of writing, it is by no means clear what will happen – the death-knell of Anglicanism as a historic church with some claim to be a national one, as opposed to a mere sect, will have sounded.

But while the Church of England was preoccupied by these legalistic and doctrinal turmoils, arising from its fundamental disunity, what of the nation? Never, it might be argued – indeed it is argued – have the people of Britain stood in more need of firm spiritual guidance from their church by law established. The need starts at the top and goes right down to the bottom. The Queen herself is beset by problems, which certainly have a spiritual dimension to them. How is she to guide her ill-behaved family into a more Christian way of life and get it to set a better example to the rest of the nation? It cannot be said that, in all her troubles, she has received the smallest effective support from her bishops. Some would say, of course, that it is the Queen who should be helping the bishops in *their* troubles, since she is still the Supreme Governor of the Church of England. Why is she not governing, indeed governing supremely? But of course the title is meaningless, or is said to be so. Again, she is *fidei defensor*, defender of the faith, or FD as her coins still inform us: why is she not defending it from the assaults of such as the Bishop of Durham? It is almost certainly true that if the Queen were to address some fierce words of rebuke to her quarrelsome or infidel bishops, and instruct them to attend to their real duties of upholding sound doctrine and morality, she would be wholeheartedly applauded, at least by the common people. It is hard to think of anything, indeed, which would make the Queen more popular. Nor is there anything, strictly speaking, to stop her intervening in this way. And the fact that she feels inhibited from doing so serves to underline, once again, how little of the spirit of democracy there is in our constitutional monarchy. But there it is. The Queen has never tried to 'tune her pulpits', as her great predecessor Elizabeth I termed it. Instead, she has silently looked to her bishops for guidance – not exactly appealing to them for succour, but expecting it – and nothing has happened.

It is the same with the nation as a whole. As crime of every kind has multiplied, as divorce has doubled and then doubled again; as the number of illegitimate births has increased to one in ten, then one in five, then one in four; as the old-style nuclear family has ceased to be the norm and in some areas especially become the exception, and many parents, or single parents, have abandoned any pretence of giving children moral training while state schools go through a formal mockery of 'religious teaching'; as the universities, followed by most of the media, have become the exponents and propagators of moral relativism and the Judeo-Christian ethic has been submerged in a jungle of permissiveness and hedonism, there has developed a growing demand among millions of ordinary people for the national clergy – the men in lawn sleeves and fancy vestments, who sport pectoral crosses and carry croziers – to speak the truth of Christian religion plainly, to denounce the wicked and exhort the righteous to action, to expound the Ten Commandments and, above all, to teach the difference between right and wrong.

It is the failure of the state church to make any perceptible response to this overwhelming demand which constitutes its huge sin of omission: a sin which is not merely a spiritual sin but a democratic sin too. The people have hungered and their pastors have not fed them. Apologists for the Anglican bishops have claimed that they routinely stress the Christian virtues and excoriate the sins of society, but their sermons are not reported: that the fault lies with the media. Not so. As a matter of fact, the Anglican church, or rather its leaders, is particularly media-conscious and skilled at getting a good hearing. It is one of the few things it is good at. Many of the bishops rose precisely because they proved themselves outstanding media-priests, sat on the right committees, produced the reports which attracted attention. While others laboured in obscure parishes, they got themselves into the headlines. Archbishop Runcie was a notable example of a prelate who rose this way.

It is not, then, that the Anglican bishops do not know how to blow the trumpet. They do. It sounds not with an uncertain note but with the wrong note. For the truth is that the successful Anglican clergy of recent decades, the ones who get the key jobs and whose views collectively constitute the Anglican voice which we all hear, comes from a tiny spectrum of opinion. It is notable for one obstinately held conviction: that responsibility is collective rather than individual and that sins are committed not primarily by people but by society. This was a commonly held view among the intelligentsia in the 1950s and 1960s when the present leaders of the church formed their views. It is the progeny of a marriage between Freudianism on the one hand and a Marxist interpretation of Christianity on the other. At bottom it is a profoundly un-Christian theory of how evil arises, for it implicitly denies that men and women are individually responsible for their actions. It thus makes nonsense of the Christian teaching of repentance and atonement and, indeed, rules out the possibility of virtue and sanctity. If no one is individually guilty how can anyone be individually meritorious? Nevertheless, for what it is worth, this is, and has been for some time, the moral theology of the Anglican leadership. Throughout the 1980s, as crime rose inexorably, Archbishop Runcie and his acolytes condemned the government. If men and women and, increasingly, children stole, it was not their fault but the responsibility of a government which encouraged greed and materialism. If men and women and, increasingly, children used violence, even killed, it was not their doing so much as a government which practised (a cant phrase of the 1980s) 'systemic violence'.

This was not, needless to say, what the people wanted to hear. After all, they were the chief victims of theft and violence and they knew very well, by bitter experience, the crimes from which they suffered were the work of sinful individuals, not society. If your car was broken into or your house burgled, how could the government be held to blame? That is the kind of syllogism which appeals to intellectuals but merely irritates ordinary people. Nonetheless, it was the direction the Church of England, or rather its leaders, chose to take. When Carey succeeded Runcie, he followed the same line, though more clumsily. When in 1992 there was an explosion of teenage violence in the Newcastle area, involving the stealing of cars which were then used in ram-raiding off-licences and other shops, in which properties were burned down and individuals seriously injured and even killed, Dr Carey blamed the government. This did not go down well even with local vicars, who found Carey's comments unhelpful (the language they used was more colourful). To the public as a whole, the episode merely confirmed the view that the Church of England could no longer be depended on to teach the moral law.

The image of the church as an irrelevance – and an increasingly embarrassing and frivolous one – was strengthened by the use senior clergy made of their matchless inheritance, the cathedrals of medieval England. In the 1970s and 1980s, it became an article of faith among some Anglican clergymen, many holding key positions, that the way to attract youth to their services was not by preaching the Gospel but by cultural bribery. The idea was to reproduce, in a church setting, the sights and sounds to which youth had become addicted by television and commercial show-business. This form of acculturalisation had sometimes been used by missionaries among tribes in Africa and the South Seas. It had not worked very well and, in Africa, had eventually led to all kinds of bastardised versions of Christianity. Now it was applied to the teenage tribes of the urban poor. On 24 April 1993, for instance, the Dean and Chapter of Winchester Cathedral held what they termed a 'rave in the nave'. Three rock bands called Cross Reference, Azimuth Brainstorm and Fresh Claim poured out deafening pop music for four hours in the magnificent stone forest, created by the master mason William of Wynford on the orders of the great William of Wykeham, Bishop of Winchester. This was preceded by a period of 'disco fun' led by the Rev. Roly Bain, described as a 'clown priest'. The Dean of Winchester, the Very Rev. Trevor Beeson, laid down the object of the occasion: 'The main thing is that the young people have a good time.' What the young people thought of the event was not recorded. What others thought was – and it began with the proposition that cathedrals do not exist so that young people, or anyone else, can 'have a good time'. This was an egregious case, but one of many, of the Anglican trumpet sounding a wrong note.

In addition to disapproval felt at the antics and attention-grabbing opinions of senior clergymen like the Bishop of Durham, there was a widespread feeling among ordinary people that the Church of England was not fully engaged in the less exciting but essential business of pastoral care. Men and women behave best where their pastors are most active. It is an undoubted fact, and a pretty obvious fact when you consider it, that the likelihood of people leading Christian lives depends in great part on whether they are persuaded to attend services regularly, say their prayers daily and come to regard specific religious activities as part of their normal routine. This kind of observance may be a bit mechanical at times but without it a true Christian community cannot exist, any more than any army can exist without discipline and drill. It was precisely in the encouragement of – the insistence upon – routine observance that Anglicanism has been weakest, even in its heyday. The example set by the clergy leaves something to be desired. Brought up as I was in a Catholic world where all priests said Mass daily if humanly possible, in addition to reading their office (which took at least an hour), I am always shocked to come across an Anglican priest who does not necessarily consider even Sunday observance incumbent upon him. I was once staying in the country in the same house as Canon John Collins, a jovial but serious-minded dignitary chiefly remarkable for his vigorous leadership of the Campaign for Nuclear Disarmament. There was no Catholic church in the neighbourhood, so on the Sunday morning I told Collins that I proposed to accompany him to the local Anglican service. 'Oh. I wasn't thinking of going, actually.' 'Not going?' 'No. I am on holiday you know'. 'But John, it's Sunday. Think of the other guests in the house. Example.' 'Oh,' crossly, 'all right then.' So we went, and the Canon, finding plenty to criticise in the sermon, cheered up in time for lunch.

It is not suggested that Anglican clergy do not work hard or fail to take their responsibilities seriously. But they do inherit the tradition of the eighteenth-century parson, not wholly eradicated by the enthusiasm of the Oxford Movement and what followed, that religion is essentially something that takes place on a Sunday. There are many aspects of Anglicanism, springing from its comfortable past as a privileged state church conducted by members of a leisured class – 'A church for gentlemen', as Charles II put it – which suggest it is more a social than a religious institution. And, now that the comfortable past is over, there is an air of bewilderment among many Anglican clergy. Church attendances have fallen dramatically in the last half-century. Many parish priests have the disheartening experience of finding a mere half-dozen elderly faces at Sunday service. Then there is the growing financial predicament. Piety and business acumen appear to be strangers in the closing decades of the twentieth century. The Roman Catholic Church expanded its resources steadily when Cardinal Spellman of New York had a hand in Vatican investment policy, 1940–60. Then came a catastrophic period when the Bank of the Holy Spirit became an international byword for gross mismanagement and worse. But most Catholic churches throughout the world are accustomed to penury and expect no better. The Anglican church is less prepared for hard times. From 1835 the church's estates were managed by the Ecclesiastical Commissioners, who in 1948 were amalgamated with the trustees of the Queen Anne's Bounty to form the Church Commissioners for England. This organisation managed the property with success, so that towards the end of the 1980s assets were calculated to be worth over £3 billion. But outgoings have been rising too. The annual total of stipends paid out to clergy (who receive an average of £12,800 a year) passed the £150-million mark in 1993, and in addition there is a pension liability of over £60 million. Then came the revelation that much of the 1980s' rise in assets was based upon high-risk property deals, which came unstuck in the early 1990s. As a result, assets fell to £2.2 billion in 1992, and early in 1994 the Church Commissioners announced they would have to halve their annual £62.7 million contribution to clergy stipends, leaving parishioners to make up the difference (they already contribute £63.6 million, according to 1992 figures).

This nasty shock raised fears for the entire future of the parish system. The Anglican church, largely run by men who have come up through the committee system, the bureaucracy and the power centres, rather than pastoral work, has built up a huge and costly administrative structure over the last half-century, while leaving parishes to fend for themselves. This has bred within the church a culture of pessimism and retrenchment, of tactical retreats and honourable surrenders. Parishes have been amalgamated, churches neglected, converted to other uses or sold off. In Norwich, for instance, once a thriving centre of Christianity with the finest collection of medieval city churches in the country, many parish churches were declared 'redundant' and handed over to a body called the Norwich Churches Trust whose function was to secularise them. Early in 1994 the religious world was shocked by the Templeman Report on Anglican churches in the City of London, which sorrowfully proposed to concentrate 'active' churches in four parishes and eight satellites, leaving twenty-seven other churches to be closed. This defeatist solution angered lovers of architecture who see it as a threat to the Wren churches which form a salient part of Anglicanism's heritage of fine buildings. But others were dismayed at further proof that the state church is giving up its evangelising role and withdrawing into an ever-contracting laager. Where will it end?

It will end, of course, in the reduction of the Church of England into an insignificant sect, because if it continues to retreat its claims to be any kind of national church will become a farce. At that point the political demand for disestablishment, as happened earlier in Ireland and Wales, will become irresistible. Once the state and legal scaffolding is removed, the existing structure will collapse. This is not just a distant prospect: it is imminent. And the plight of the established church affects other institutions, notably the monarchy. 'No bishop, no king' – James I's warning is still relevant. Oxford and Cambridge will be likewise shaken as will many great public schools, like Eton, Winchester and

Westminster. The fall of the Church of England will have reverberations throughout the ancient fabric of the country.

To whom can the church turn? To God, of course. But God helps those who help themselves. And in its plight, Anglicanism has no other resource but the people. There are, happily, many millions of professing Christians still in Britain, and many millions more who, consciously or not, believe in the Judeo-Christian ethic, in the morality of the Decalogue and in the need for a set of absolute values. Some look to the Catholic Church, some to the nonconformist churches, others to Judaism for their regular guidance. But many are still habituated to think of themselves as 'C of E' and would gladly transform that vague allegiance into an active profession of faith if they were offered a bit of inspiration from the men in lawn sleeves. And most would rejoice if the Church of England, taking advantage of its privileged position in the nation's life, were to roll up those sleeves and become a church militant again. At present, the masses look for spiritual sustenance and they are given not bread but a politically correct stone. There is a huge hunger waiting to be satisfied. Christianity in England – indeed in Britain – is not dead, it is not even moribund. It is starved, undernourished, suffering from chronic malnutrition. There are countless Christian people queuing up impatiently for the square meal of ancient truth, preached by men – yes, and women too – who have stout hearts, strong faith, firm voices and the light of battle in their eyes, and who are not daunted when the chattering classes, always on the cynical watch, label them 'fundamentalists'. That could be a proud badge in a country whose people long to be told, in the authoritative tones of the ordained clergy led by their bishops, the age-old difference between right and wrong. But can Anglicanism, on its sick bed – perhaps its death bed – find its voice at last?

CHAPTER TEN

A Well-Aimed Gobbet of Spit
in the Public's Eye

If religion is not just something which is done on Sunday, nor is culture a mere luxury. The two are linked, as is indicated by the common French word *culte*, worship. There is a strong element of spirituality in both, and men and women need the spiritual as much as they need food, water and shelter. There is a longing to be filled with awe, to experience the numinous, the sublime. No one with any sense of justice would deny religion to the common people. It was precisely because the Judaism of the first century AD seemed so inaccessible to the uninstructed, illiterate *Am Ha-Aretz*, 'the people of the land', that Jesus Christ offered them his New Testament. And who would be so cruel as to seek to deprive the people of culture? Yet it happens, all the time, in the closing years of the twentieth century. We live in a society where there is a systematic contrivance of the self-elect to define culture in terms which make it inaccessible to the commonalty.

This is a blow struck at the core of a nation. One reason why the British are so downhearted and take so dispirited a view of their country's predicament is that so many of them are cut off, and feel themselves cut off, from the oxygen of culture. They are not content with the quotidian pabulum of television, cable, videos, pop music, tabloids: they know there is an enchantment missing from their lives, and that the deprivation is not their fault but is in some way the responsibility of those in authority. It is another failure of democracy. One could argue it is the most dismal failure of all because a people without culture are not a real nation, just an aggregate of bewildered individuals. Dr Johnson once observed that in the long run peoples are remembered for their writers, above all their poets, or they are not remembered at all. It matters nothing to us that the city-states of Greece once lorded it over the Mediterranean. All we care about are the precious fragments of their literature and art which, by some miracle, have survived. We take little interest now in Le Roi Soleil and his glory, in his victories and defeats. But Molière still lives for us. Frederick the Great's chief claim to distinction now is that he was the friend of Voltaire.

A true culture which is also a popular culture is a potent source of national morale. During that great explosion of British energy, genius, wealth, adventure, aggression and conquest which marked the eighteenth century, when we launched the Industrial Revolution, created a world empire and kept the flame of freedom burning brightly for all Europe to see, John Bull fed heartily on the national culture. London at mid-century was in some ways a cruel and barbarous place. Grub Street was a hungry reality and even Samuel Johnson sometimes walked the city at night because he had not a shilling in his pocket. But culture was on tap even for those who could scarcely afford a square meal – culture they could taste and relish. George Frederick Handel's *Music for the Royal Fireworks* was thumped out in 1748 before a seething, smelly mob of tens of thousands in Green Park, his *Messiah* (1742) was sung regularly in a dozen City churches. James Thomson's *The Seasons* (1730) was read by the nation as a whole and recited in taverns as well as in drawing rooms. There were few who did not know a few lines of Pope – often hundreds – and countless people learned by heart the moving verses of Gray's *Elegy* when it was published in 1751. William Hogarth, our first great native painter, was a do-it-yourself artistic entrepreneur, who ran his own gallery and art school, sold his paintings by public auction, engraved his own plates and marketed the results, hawking subscriptions and ensuring his satires were in every shop window. Even an illiterate crossing-sweeper, clearing the mud and horse dung from the steps of the gentry, knew what was going on. On the night of 12 September 1759, as General James Wolfe was being rowed down the St Lawrence to storm the Heights of Abraham, he recited Gray's *Elegy* to the crew and soldiers on his longboat, and when they murmured their appreciation he said: 'I would rather be the author of that piece than take Quebec.' In the eighteenth century Britain was not yet a democracy. Only about 800,000 men had the vote. But in a cultural sense it was a democracy of sorts already.

You may ask: what has democracy to do with the arts? The answer is, a great deal. The essence of democracy is the ability of ordinary people to influence what happens. They can do this in a number of different ways; most notably, in constitutional terms, by their votes. But probably the most effective way, if the truth be told, is through their purses. They vote in the ballot box only once every four or five years. But they vote with their purses every day of their lives. That is why markets are so important to human freedom – that is, if they are true markets and not rigged ones. Great art can be created in many different fashions. But the surest way in which art will reflect and express and heighten the sensibilities of the time is through the market. The artist displays his wares. The patron pays for them. Or the patron commands, suggests, coaxes, pleads. The artist responds, in his fashion. The cash nexus is the guarantee of the artist's livelihood. It is the guarantee, too, that people care for the arts enough to pay for them, out of their own pockets: they put their money where their mouths are. And, finally, it is the guarantee that the artist earns his living honestly, like everyone else.

Shakespeare was a characteristic product of market democracy. He worked for a company which was patronised by a great man, called after him indeed. The great man provided protection from puritanical City Fathers, or prod-nosed clergy. He ensured his players did not get into trouble by imprudent comment. Sometimes he dipped into his pocket on the company's behalf. But in general the players lived by the box office. Shakespeare might write *Love's Labour's Lost*, with its countless 'in' references, for a Court audience, but in general his works had to play to full houses of ordinary theatregoers to justify their place in the repertoire. In 1601 the Essex plotters, as part of the propaganda build-up to their rising, engaged Shakespeare's company, the Lord Chamberlain's Men, to put on a special afternoon performance of *Richard II*, which was an old play but showed a king being dethroned. The company's manager, Augustine Phillips, later told the Privy Council:

> We were determined to have played some other play, as we held that play of King Richard to be so old and so long out of use as that we should have small or no company at it. But at their request we were content to play it the Saturday and had our forty shilling more than our ordinary for it.

In other words, they got £2 on top of the price of tickets for filling the whole house. Shakespeare knew very well, as he made clear in two magical speeches by Hamlet, that 'the groundlings', who were given no seating and only paid a penny entrance, were 'capable of nothing but inexplicable dumb-show and noise'. Too 'excellent' a play might be 'caviare to the general'. On the other hand, he qualified his criticism of the groundlings by admitting that even some of them might appreciate quality, and anyway their pennies, like the tuppences and sixpences of the better seats, helped to pay the company's salaries and bills. He provided enough dumb-shows and noise to keep their patronage. There are a thousand indications in his texts that he sought hard to give honest entertainment as well as great art to the whole spectrum of his audience.

A classic example of the democratic cultural market at work is provided by the reception of *The Pickwick Papers* when it appeared in monthly parts in 1837. Charles Dickens was already a professional writer but unknown to the general public, and the series was originally planned round the illustrator, who already had a following. As John Forster tells us, there was no 'newspaper notice or puffing' at all for the first five numbers. They sold entirely on their merit; the public picked them up, bought and read them, and told their friends. By the fifth number, said Forster, 'people talked of nothing else' and 'tradesmen recommended their goods by using its name'. The print run jumped from 400 for the first number to 40,000 for the fifteenth. It appealed to all classes, from errand-boys to the august. Carlyle told what he called a 'dreadful story' of an archdeacon who 'had been administering ghostly consolation to a sick person [and] having finished, satisfactorily as he thought, and got out of the room, he heard the sick person ejaculate: "Well, thank God, *Pickwick* will be out in ten days anyway!'"

There is something immensely satisfying about a work charging to success on the unassisted backs of ordinary readers. J. B. Priestley told me about what happened to his novel *The Good Companions* in 1929: 'I finished it in March – 250,000 words. I thought it ordinary, good, brass-and-mahogany work, nothing special. Heinemann brought it out in July and felt they were pretty daring printing 10,000 copies. Nobody much boosted it, middling reviews, not much advertising. By the end of August it had sold 7,500 – not bad. Then the word began to get around – "It's a good read." Wall Street collapsed. Maybe people wanted cheering up. Anyway, by Christmas Heinemann were delivering 5,000 copies a day to the London bookshops by van.' Word of mouth – the cultural market – made it one of the top sellers of the century. I saw this happen again, myself, with John Braine's *Room at the Top* in 1957. It had been around a dozen publishers before my friend John Raymond bough it for Eyre and Spottiswoode. He told me: 'I'm not sure I really approve of this book but it is a work of art and a humdinger.' He did manage to get pre-publication endorsements from Walter Allen and C. P. Snow, but neither was particularly well-known, and that was all. The book took off by itself simply because the ordinary reader enjoyed it and sang its praises to others.

Now, a generation later, the market has been taken out of the hands of the general reading public. It is manipulated by publicists and PR experts of every kind, by highly-paid 'marketing managers', by television pluggers and the radio salesmen. Astronomical advances are paid by publishers for 'guaranteed bestsellers' which are hailed as masterpieces even before they are written, let alone available to readers. The reader is no longer trusted to make up his own mind: he is subjected to the hard sell. A few men and women in deep-carpeted offices have stolen cultural democracy from him. To cap it all, we now have the most non-democratic, indeed anti-democratic, device of all: the prize system. This was invented

by the Goncourt brothers, who wanted their memory per-
petuated and to enjoy a renown which their novels and plays
had never quite won in their lifetimes. It involved creating a
self-perpetuating 'academy' of literary fashion-mongers and
know-alls. It was modelled on the Académie Française,
appointed under Louis XIV to exercise a subtle control over
French intellectual life, and which has had, over the centuries, a
remarkably deadening effect on the most gifted people in the
world. The Goncourt Academy was set up in 1903 and began to
give an annual prize to the best work of prose, usually a novel,
published in France the previous year. Earlier juries occasionally picked a winner: they gave the prize in 1919 to Proust's *A
l'ombre des jeunes filles en fleurs*. They also took account of public
opinion, at least from time to time. Thus in 1933 they awarded
the prize to André Malraux's *La Condition humaine*. But
gradually the Goncourt was imitated by other prizes, and
publishers began to gear their industry to the system, plugging
the winners to the limit of their resources – and ignoring the
others. A seat on a jury was no longer an invitation to select
and award merit, but a right to distribute patronage, or follow
fashion, or exercise political prejudice or personal whim. The
juries were composed essentially of other writers, or
intellectuals, about the last people on earth who ought to be
given power over their fellows. By the 1950s the deleterious
effects of the system were already detectable and by the 1990s
the French novel has become virtually a dead form of great
art.

Despite the damage inflicted by the prize system on French
literature, it was adopted here in the 1920s, and hugely
commercialised when the Booker McConnell Prize was set up
for novels in 1969. It got off to a slow start but sensationalised
itself by becoming the occasion for a television jamboree. This
combined all the evils of television with the evils of literary
élitism and fashion. It took the novel out of the hands of the
reading public and put it where it should never belong, in the
pockets of the chattering classes, who had too much power
already. When the Booker had been going a decade or so, I
protested strongly against this huge addition to their
patronage. The chairman of Booker McConnell came to

see me and asked what he should do to put things right. I made my point about the importance of democracy in culture and said that, if it were impossible to have the best novel selected by the entire reading public, at least the jury should be composed of ordinary people familiar with the art – English teachers, librarians, booksellers and a few readers selected at random. He was horrified by the idea. I suppose he felt that one object of his firm putting up a large sum of prize money and paying for a big party was to enable members of his board and their wives to mingle with the top literary nobs in front of the television cameras. They would not take kindly to mingling with municipal librarians and suchlike humble folk. Oh no, said he, he was hoping to get from me suggestions about 'fine tuning' the Booker Prize, but my proposal would 'ruin the idea'.

So the Booker and other prizes have continued to knock golden nails into the coffin of English literature. These prizes have become the occasion for exercises in grotesque political bias, positive discrimination, national masochism, internationalism at its worst, political correctness and sheer fashion. Literature has averted her bowed head, weeping. I once asked a student of prize form what were the ideal qualifications for winning the Booker. He replied: 'Be a woman, preferably a lesbian; non-white, that is, East Asian, South Asian, Middle Eastern, Caribbean, African, in ascending order of desirability; hone your prose style on the taste of NW1, NW3 and W11; and, as for subject-matter, direct a well-aimed gobbet of spit straight in the public's eye.'

A light-hearted survey of great nineteenth-century novelists suggests that it would be hard to pick a Booker winner. Scott? 'Traditionalist euphoria and schoolboy nostalgia.' Jane Austen? 'She writes exclusively about ladies and gentlemen.' Dickens? 'Adolescent emotionalism, tear-jerking and crime-doesn't-pay obscurantism. Anti-Semitic, too.' Charlotte Brontë? 'Wedding-bell endings and heterosexual triumphalism.' Thackeray? 'White male chauvinism and social snobbery.' George Eliot? 'It's true she lived in sin with G. H. Lewes. On the other hand, the novels are all about Victorian values.' Henry James? 'Yankee imperialist and the workers never get a look-in.' Joseph Conrad? 'You must be joking. Are you

seriously suggesting we could give the Booker to a man who
called one of his novels *The Nigger of the Narcissus*?' The only
conceivable winner among the Victorians would have been
George Meredith. Mannered, 'literary' and endlessly boosted
by a clique who eventually succeeded in making his sales
respectable, he has since sunk without trace. There indeed we
have Booker material.

The quintessential Booker novelist, the instant-best seller
and pre-packaged giant-of-literature writer is, of course,
Salman Rushdie, who not merely won the Booker Prize but
was eventually judged, quite rightly in a way, to be the Booker
Prize winner *par excellence*. When his novel *Midnight's Children*
won the prize, I bought a copy. The fact that, despite reading
it front-to-back, back-to-front, sideways and even upside
down, I could make no sense of it at all, first alerted me to the
menace of Bookerism. Rushdie, of course, might have been
designed to fit the Booker specifications. It is true he is not a
woman. On the other hand, he is not just non-white but
studiously so. And, whatever he may lack in literary
articulation, his ability to direct that gobbet of spit is up
to Bisley standard. That, of course, is what attracted the
judges to him in the first place, the sheer venom-content,
directed at officially designated targets like the Tories, the
police, etc. Unfortunately for Rushdie, thus encouraged, he
sent a well-aimed gobbet of spit straight into the eye of the
Ayatollah Khomeini.

Rushdie's subsequent misfortunes raise an illuminating
point. The behaviour of the Iranian régime, in sentencing him
to death and egging on its more fanatical adherents to carry
out the *fatwa*, is outrageous. If it had been issued against a
genuine, publicly recognised giant of English literature,
against a Tennyson, say, or a Kipling or even a T. S. Eliot, the
public rage would have been overwhelming. If Teheran had,
for instance, condemned Sir John Betjeman to death, I really
think it might have been a case for sending in the gunboats.
But Rushdie is a Booker giant of literature, and that is not the
same thing. The Foreign Office has wearily gone through the
motions of protest. The police have dutifully supplied the
protection. The taxpayers have resentfully paid for it. A

ragged chorus of literary busybodies have periodically given tongue. But the public has displayed almost total indifference. That is what is liable to happen when you take democracy out of culture.

Indeed, it is possible to detect in the public's attitude to many cultural manifestations today not merely rejection – a feeling that what is produced has absolutely no relevance to their lives, no correspondence with their taste and nothing to do with their idea of what constitutes art – but a rising resentment. There is a common belief among ordinary people that culture – that is, not what they would call culture but what 'They' call culture – is heavily subsidised and that most of the money is thrown away. And there is some truth in this view. The days when Sir Kenneth Clark coaxed an embattled government into providing a few hundred thousand pounds to keep the arts alive in war-torn London are a long way in the past. The sums are routinely denounced by the various culture lobbies as niggardly and philistine but they seem to ordinary people to be Babylonian. The National Heritage budget for 1994 is £980 million and will certainly be over a billion next year. It is true that some of this goes on preserving castles and other buildings which the public loves to visit. Some also goes on keeping the Royal Opera up to the standard expected by visiting dignitaries. The public sees this as a necessary evil, though it draws in its breath when told that performances are subsidised at the rate of £50 a seat. But a goodly portion of this vast annual budget does indeed go on paying for what most people regard as rubbish, sometimes nasty, pernicious and dirty rubbish. Once art begins to be paid for by the taxpayers it is amazing how quickly the more arcane forms of sexuality make their appearance. But even when subsidised art is innocuous, it has that gobbet-of-spit quality, and the public does not enjoy having to wipe its eye *and* pay for the experience. There are two items which are particularly remembered. The first was, is, the display of firebricks at the Tate Gallery. Sensible people do not automatically condemn manifestations of modern art. Surprisingly often they are prepared to give the artist the benefit of the doubt. But simple firebricks presented as high art was an open-and-shut case of twaddle. After all, some people have to work with firebricks to earn a living. They can make an arrangement themselves. So they knew they were being conned. The second case occurred when the Arts Council paid two men to carry a plank around East Anglia. Whence they started, where they went, how long they carried the plank and what it stood for slipped from the public's memory. But the image of the men and the plank stuck and came to symbolise the whole business of taxpayer's money keeping modern art going.

The public can show their resentment at what is being done to them in various ways. One is by displaying total apathy. This, in general, has been the line taken in dealing with modern music. No effort has been spared by the elites, for more than half a century, to force dissonance, atonality and other forms of modernism into the public's ears. If there had been any real merit in it, the public would have responded or at least developed Pavlovian reflexes. Sometimes, of course, they do not have much choice in the matter. If the Controller of Radio Three gives them an unrelieved diet of Schönberg, or worse, they have no alternative but to switch off. Correction: Now they do have an alternative: to switch to Classic FM, and many have done precisely that – an admirable example of how, the moment monopoly is replaced by the market, democracy perks up again. Where the public has a choice, by purchasing seats, their preferences become plain. It is a significant indicator that, whereas in 1820, say, over 90 per cent of the music played in concert halls and opera houses in Vienna, Dresden, Paris, Rome, Milan and other European centres was contemporary, that is written by living composers or those recently dead, and whereas this proportion was kept up throughout the nineteenth century and even up to 1914, it has now been reversed. The 10 per cent which is written by living composers is heard on sufferance and has to be balanced by old favourites in the programme.

There was a typical example of active apathy not long ago at the Royal Festival Hall when a noisy work by Sir Harrison Birtwistle had its first performance. I mean no disrespect to Sir Harrison. He is no worse than any other modern composer; he may, indeed, be better than many. I cite him merely as an example. This new work was sugared by the main item, a rare performance of Mahler's so-called Tenth Symphony. This, though popularly known as 'The Interminable', is a definite attraction. Sir Harrison's work was performed first, and after it was over there was polite applause. Sir Harrison was present and moved hastily towards the stage to receive his ovation. Alas, even before he had scrambled onto it and shaken the conductor's hand, the applause had begun to falter, and it was only the phlegmatic decency of the English music-lover which accorded him a few more claps. When democracy can work, it gives the taste of the self-appointed élites the thumbs down. But rejection is negative. We have still lost half a century or more of real musical history, and this is one reason why British music-lovers, who after all were sufficiently adventurous to sponsor Beethoven's Ninth Symphony in the 1820s, are dejected.

Dejection is the characteristic mood of a society where the people are alienated from the culture of the day, and where its manifestations are not occasions for joy but felt to be symbols of oppression by a minority in power. Sometimes these symbols are gigantic as well as oppressive, so large they fill the horizon and are inescapable. Art can uplift, soothe, reassure, inspire and edify: those are its normal functions. It can also, directly or subconsciously, incite and brutalise. One factor contributing to the growing violence, insensitivity and sheer barbarism of our society is modern architecture, with its crude, pseudo-functional lines, coarse use of materials like concrete and steel, absence of ornament and deliberate cult of gracelessness. Propagated by sinister ideologues like Le Corbusier, whose very definition of a house as 'a machine for living in' betrayed his aim to dehumanise architecture, it dominated the field for the entire third quarter of the twentieth century. Indeed, it still controls the architectural establishments of most Western countries. In Britain it made its appearance in a particularly debased form. Indeed, looking at the way in which it has ravished entire towns and cities, once crowded with fine buildings from earlier, more genial ages, I am sometimes inclined to sympathise with the outraged art-lover who insisted, not long ago, 'All architects should be executed, on principle.' (It should come as no surprise to learn that in

Belgium, another victim, '*architecte*' is an actionable term of abuse.)

Today there is no form of artistic expression over which ordinary people have less control than architecture. Only an insignificant minority of rich people have the means to employ architects themselves. So the market scarcely works at all. Most architectural commissions are awarded by tiny committees on behalf of the state, local government, huge corporations and other anonymous bodies, spending other people's money, not their own, and therefore easily swayed by ideological fashion. The people feel they have no alternative but to submit to what is built around them. It has often been suggested that the design of modern housing estates, reflecting the whims of architectural trend-followers rather than human needs, is one explanation for the crime which engulfs them. To create these monstrosities, countless thousands of agreeable Victorian, Edwardian and Georgian terraced houses, which could easily have been modernised and which lined real, neighbourly streets, were bulldozed. Some of the architects who built these hells actually boasted of their savagery and called their style the New Brutalism. It is not surprising their work incited people to crime, as well as making it easy.

It is not only council tenants who have been debased by modern architecture. We all have. Buildings are not things you can take or leave. We can avert our gaze from modern sculpture or painting, we can refuse to go to cacophonous concerts, we can leave books we find ridiculous or offensive on the shelves. By merely turning a knob we can isolate ourselves from the entire world of broadcasting. But buildings we cannot escape. They tower over us, grab us by the arm as we hurry through the streets as if to say: 'Hey you, I'm here, huge and hideous, there's no getting away from *me*!' In a city like Bristol, once magnificent, there is now no vista not ruined by the savage artifacts of modernism. If you go to the end of the pier at Brighton, you can see before you the entire spread of what was once the finest Regency city in the world, like a brilliant smile of white ivory, but with some of the teeth cruelly wrenched out, as if by an insane dentist, and replaced by modernistic molars, out-of-scale and already rotten. Even in the centre of Hyde

Park, London's gracious *rus in urbe* – planned to be like the true countryside with only distant village steeples rising above the treeline – there is now no escaping the high oblong insults of the Hilton hotel, the Knightsbridge Barracks and other pallid slabs. All of us, everywhere, are constantly, almost imperceptibly, incited to murderous thoughts. Every morning, as I look out on my quiet early Victorian London street, with its trim and delightful pairs of white stucco 1840 villas, I am tempted to crime by the sight opposite where, in lax pre-war days, an architect called Denys Lasdun was allowed to pull down two of them and build an offensive box. That box is now, I do not doubt, listed. The architectural establishment, with fine contempt for ordinary people, has recently bullied the government into slapping preservation orders on many of the worst excesses of the 1960s and 1970s, so we are stuck with them for ever.

It is true that the people, thus surrounded by oppressive skylines, can seek the solace of beauty in our art galleries, where the works of earlier, wiser ages are on display. But even there their choice is limited by the anti-democratic whims of the élites. The Tate Gallery which, by an unfortunate dispensation, houses the national collections both of British and of Modern Art, crowds its cellars with fine paintings and sculptures produced and cherished by our ancestors, in order to make space for firebricks and the like. There, the walls and floors are kept in a constant state of modernistic flux as its masterful director, Nicholas Serota, arranges and rearranges 'his' properties, so that provincial art-lovers, in London on a rare visit and hoping to see an old Tate favourite, are liable to be disappointed. They have to be content with what the Brickies, as the mandarins of modern art are now called, think good for them.

The power of these placemen over our visual lives is frightening. Serota, the Brickie-in-Chief, not only presides over the Tate, whose collection has doubled since the 1950s – at the time of writing it owns 4055 paintings, 1050 sculptures and 30,000 works on paper – but now controls an offshoot in St Ives and another in Liverpool. He is also chairman of the judges of the Turner Prize, the most publicised of the art awards and the visual equivalent of the Booker. The Turner is notorious for ejecting gobbets of spit at the public, being awarded one year to two moon-faced homosexuals whose joint work of art is, apparently, themselves. In 1993 Serota and his fellow-judges gave the prize to a plaster cast of an East London house. This derisive, or ironic, or in any event insensitive, comment on the housing of the poor by a well-to-do middle-class artist merely involved the mechanical manipulation of large quantities of concrete. Ordinary East Enders did not understand why the woman responsible should be awarded £20,000 for it. One of them scrawled on it 'Wot For?' and Tower Hamlets council made its feelings clear by demolishing the thing, to the cheers of the populace. It would be hard to think of a more apt demonstration of the undemocratic nature of Brickie art.

It is worth noting that making plaster casts of ordinary objects and displaying them as 'art' is not new. Far from it. When modern art first breached the boundaries of presentation, reason and common sense in the early 1920s, every conceivable gimmick was deployed. By 1925 Dadaists and the like were already running out of ideas with which to *épater le bourgeois*. Recent manifestations of Brickie art, such as cascades of toilet paper and walls of chocolate, are old, old hat. Modern Art, far from being fresh, adventurous, daring, innovative, shocking or creative – all the adjectives the Brickies employ so lavishly – is not even new. In all its essential aspects, it is nearly a century old. It is one of the longest-drawn-out movements in the history of art and is now sustained and prolonged very largely by money. So much has been invested by galleries, public and private, by curators and directors and dealers that they feel they simply cannot afford to let the imposture founder. Equally, critics and experts and academics, publishers and art magazines, have invested their images and reputations in the racket. They are identified with it, and if it is swept away they will go too.

Yet this is increasingly likely to happen and probably quite soon. Democracy cannot be held at bay indefinitely, even in the realm of culture. There are premonitory signs. Drawing is once more being taught in some art schools. Among the young, there is a resurgence of what the Brickies insultingly categorise as 'representational' painters, but what most people would call 'proper' painters. And some fine old painters who had given up in despair are beginning to exhibit again, and sell their works. This is a huge delight to collectors like myself. For many years I bought works only from the eighteenth or nineteenth centuries, or by pre-war artists, all of them dead. Now in the last year or so alone I have been able to patronise a dozen living painters. I believe other, similar collectors are girding their loins and opening up their purses. There is a new spirit abroad, and the world is opening up to young men and women of talent who have keen eyes, skilled hands and a love of nature and humanity.

The Brickies are already worried by this democratic in-surgence. They hear the angry murmurs of the people and they tremble in their seats of power. Recently, the Tate felt it had to bring out its own magazine, called of course *tate*, as a defensive measure. In London there are, at the time of writing, fewer than half a dozen art critics who are not part of or sympathetic to the Brickie racket. One of them, with a particularly broad know-ledge of the history of art, including the modern movement, and an unusually sharp pen is Brian Sewell of the London *Evening Standard*. The Brickies hate him with a passion which has to be heard to be believed. In January 1994 a lynch party of them – gallery owners and minor curators, art academics, BBC people, writers and cultural busybodies – wrote a joint letter to the *Standard* calling for Sewell to be disciplined. They termed themselves 'Members of the Art World' as though it were a kind of exclusive club, like the Garrick, from which the rest of us can be blackballed. Nothing could have demonstrated more clearly the undemocratic attitude of the people who, until recently at least, have completely dominated the world of contemporary painting and sculpture. And it is a sign of the times that this letter had the opposite effect of what was intended. It turned Sewell, a retiring, scholarly recluse, into a national figure, whose defiant television appearances evoked cheers from the despised *hoi polloi*. Indeed, it launched a public debate which is running heavily against the Brickies and which still continues.

Alas, the damage inflicted over the last half-century or more, in this and other fields of culture, cannot be put right simply by belated victories. The marks of cultural deprivation and malnutrition are permanent. We have brought up entire generations of children into a barren age. There is one particular area where the tragedy is truly heart-rending: poetry. If Britain is famous for anything, it is for its poetry. The Germans have produced the best philosophers and musicians, the Russians the finest novelists, the Italians and Dutch the greatest painters, the French a whole range of supreme artists in fields ranging from furniture and architecture to porcelain. But we have the poets: our island has indeed been a 'nest of singing birds'. They stretch in majestic succession from Chaucer to T. S. Eliot, scarcely one generation without a master, often with several. The sheer richness of our poetry has never been equalled. In the years after Waterloo, for example, Scott, Byron, Shelley, Keats, Crabbe, Coleridge, Wordsworth, Lamb and Leigh Hunt – to name only the best known – were all producing poetry. What a galaxy of genius! Poetry has been the special privilege and delight of British youth. There was a time, not so long ago, when no schoolboy or schoolgirl of any ambition would get to the sixth form without pouring out sonnets or even blank-verse plays. I recall trying a five-acter while one of my sisters was hard at work on an epic. This was not at all unusual. And even those who did not write poetry learned it. Teenagers left school knowing by heart thousands, sometimes tens of thousands of lines of poetry, of all kinds. I used to be able to recite virtually the whole of the Prologue to Chaucer's *Canterbury Tales*. That was not unusual either. *Hamlet* soliloquies, entire odes by Keats and Shelley, majestic chunks of *Paradise Lost* and *The Prelude, Kubla Khan, The Rime of the Ancient Mariner* and *The Idylls of the King* – all that was nothing.

Now most children seem to leave school not only without having written a single line of poetry but without knowing one either. The loss is outrageous and of course irreparable. It is a moral as well as a cultural loss. Recently, a senior Conservative MP, a member of the 1922 Committee, revealed (or perhaps I should say boasted) that he had never read any poetry in his life. It is not quite clear what point he was trying to make with this startling announcement. It may be that he was intending a comment on the present deplorable state of poetry, or on the educational system. Or perhaps he was trying to bolster a macho image of himself. At all events, one believed him. It is now not only possible but even likely that many people will go through life without reading any poetry. If poetry ceases to be a contemporary art with wide appeal, then the poets of the past will eventually be neglected too. This is already happening.

Who is most responsible for this calamity is not easy to determine. One can blame, first, the poets who have imbibed ever-deeper draughts of cultural egotism and written increasingly to please themselves rather than their readers. Or one can blame the critics, editors and academics who have encouraged them in this suicidal course, and hailed poets and poems precisely because they are 'difficult' or 'inaccessible'. Entire academic industries have been erected on the incomprehensible. Poets no less than painters, novelists and musicians are easily corrupted, misled, egged on to greater folly by those who praise impudence. Poetry too has been further demoralised by the prize system. In poetry, the equivalent of the Booker or Turner is the Forward Poetry Prize. It was awarded in 1993 to Carol Ann Duffy. I am sorry to say I had never heard of her. Had you, reader? There is a fierce little literary industry called poetry-writing which takes place in a kind of ghetto of its own, cut off from the rest of the population completely. A few poets like Betjeman and Wendy Cope have leapt over the ghetto wall, but most fester inside. The public are put off by what little they know of their wares. The most admired poet of recent years, living in Hull amid a litter of jazz records and soft-porn magazines, celebrating misogyny, Little Englandism and masturbation, is known only for three lines: 'They f— you up, your Mum and Dad'; and 'Sexual intercourse began / In nineteen sixty-three'. It would be hard to decide what characterises them more, inelegance or falsehood. If this is poetry, say some, then we are better off without it. Yet that is the resignation of despair. We can breed new generations of poets when the people take the power back into their hands. But we must start soon.

CHAPTER ELEVEN

Egalitarian Nightmares
and Clanging Alarm-Bells

*W*hat is the solution to Britain's miseries? Democratic leadership. Or, to put it another way, more democracy, better leadership. Winston Churchill once said that democracy was a bad form of government but that all the alternatives were worse. True, but negative. Democracy can be an admirable form of government given strong, popular leadership which ensures that the voice of the people is translated into practical measures and realistic policies.

It is sometimes urged that democracy and leadership are incompatible and that democracy is meaningless unless all are equal. Nothing could be further from the truth. The people hate equality. They know by instinct that it is unattainable. They are the first to suffer from misguided attempts to promote it. What they want is equality before the law and equality of opportunity. These are the preconditions of a good society. A democracy works best when it is run on merit. A society where the ruling class is open to all talents, where social mobility is encouraged and where men and women rise by their industry and skill is the most likely to function successfully and give satisfaction to all its members.

Britain is not such a society today – far from it. That is why it functions badly and its people are unhappy. Herein lies a tragedy, and a historical anomaly too, because Britain has been great in the past precisely because it was a country where the able could get to the top whatever their origins. The great

Thomas Becket started as a scrivener's clerk, William of Wykeham, whose munificence created Winchester and New College, as a kennel-boy, Cardinal Wolsey, the founder of Christ Church, Oxford, as a butcher's assistant. Drake's father was a humble 'reader of prayers', Admiral Blake's a farmer, Captain Cook's a labourer, Lord Chancellor Eldon's a coal-heaver, Nelson's a country parson. Ramsay MacDonald, Britain's first Labour Prime Minister, was the son of an unmarried mother. So was Ernest Bevin, who began life as a farmer's lad and rose to be one of Britain's greatest Foreign Secretaries. The world's first industrial revolution was pushed through in Britain largely by the children of the poor or the humble. In Britain, lowly birth has never been a bar to the top. Nor has high birth. Churchill had to face many obstacles before he led the country, but being the grandson of a duke was not one of them. The genius of Britain has been to recognise talent wherever it is found. It is a significant fact that the Tories, the party of birth, were the first to bestow their leadership on the son of an actress, a converted Jew and a woman.

Given this true and tested tradition of empiricism, it is heart-breaking to observe how, in recent decades, Britain has turned its back on meritocracy and freedom, to embrace compulsory and self-defeating social engineering. Of course when I say Britain I do not mean the British people. I mean, rather, the unrepresentative and usually unelected groups who have perverted the democratic process and imposed their ideology on the rest. The people never voted for a system of welfare dependency but that is what they have got: and dependency is a social disease which might have been designed to strangle the initiative and adventurism of the poor and prevent their talents and genius manifesting themselves. This proposition applies to all, but almost certainly more to women than to men.

Nor did the people ever vote for the levelling process in education. What they wanted was more opportunity, not more equality. The destruction of the grammar schools carried out by Labour governments and acquiesced in by the Conservatives, was the greatest act of vandalism in Britain since the civil war. It ended a meritocratic tradition which went back to the

Dark Ages. Even in King Alfred's day a clever village boy would be spotted by the parish priest, taken into a monastic school and bred for the highest service in church and state. When monasticism was ended in the mid-sixteenth century its educational role was taken over by the new grammar schools, which for hundreds of years gave clever boys from humble homes – and, increasingly, in the last century, girls too – the best schooling available and enabled them to work their way to the top. Some grammar schools were better than others – a few were among the best schools in the world – but all insisted on hard work, strict discipline and the pursuit of excellence. Their replacement by the comprehensive school was a disaster for working-class high-flyers.

The notion that the poor oppose meritocracy and benefit from its suppression is false. Poor people admire talent and industry as much as anyone else and rejoice to see it fairly rewarded, especially when it comes from their own ranks. In North Staffordshire, when I was a boy, an entire street would celebrate when a boy or a girl from it got into a grammar school and, still more, won a place at university. Such success was a spur to others to work hard too, and the parents knew it. In the moorland villages on the fringe of the Potteries, scholarship boys and girls were local heroes and heroines. There were many different kinds of scholarships in those days, some of great antiquity, provided by the wills of pious benefactors, often themselves self-made men or their widows. Local authorities added to the total with awards significantly termed 'open scholarships'. Then there were state scholarships, another tier. One way or another they ensured that the best and the brightest got right up the educational ladder. The strong motivation encouraged by the scholarship system induced a striving competitiveness which remained with the beneficiaries throughout life. Margaret Thatcher, a slightly older contemporary of mine, is a characteristic example of the breed. She has scholarship girl written all over her, even to this day. She will be competing on her deathbed for the Best Last Words.

In the post-war world the right strategy would have been to increase the number of awards, beginning by widening the places available to the poor at every kind of educational establishment, including the public schools and Oxbridge. This would have been fully in accord with the intentions of the pious founders of these establishments. More grammar schools should have been built. Instead the movement was all the other way. Not only were grammar schools subsumed in egalitarian colossi, where discipline rapidly deteriorated, but many local authorities ceased to award scholarships to boarding schools. A future Labour government pledged itself, in February 1994, to outlaw such awards. Every encouragement has been given to class warfare, bitterness and envy, every discouragement to education for its own sake.

It is surely significant that, over the last half-century, parents of bright children, and those most anxious to do everything humanly possible to get their offspring good educations – precisely the sort of parents whose enthusiasm is most valuable to society and who ought to be given the maximum encouragement by the state – have increasingly turned to the fee-paying rather than the state system. They have sacrificed holidays, clothes, cars and savings in order to find the school fees. The knowledge that this is happening has been bitterly resented by the ideologues and social engineers who hold high positions in the policy-forming levels of education and swarm over the universities. At Oxford and, still more, at Cambridge, for instance, it is now not only common but usual for dons selecting entrants to exclude systematically boys and girls from fee-paying schools, irrespective of their educational attainments. Some colleges boycott certain famous schools, like Eton, Winchester and Westminster, altogether. The same conspiracy – that is what it amounts to – is beginning to operate against famous girls' schools like Roedean and Cheltenham Ladies College. The justification for this wicked system is that, hitherto, the rich have been able to 'buy' places at famous universities for their children simply by paying for them to go to good boarding schools. But that is a political accusation rather than a serious argument and, even if it were true in some cases, it ignores the fact that most children at fee-paying schools do not have rich parents. They are fortunate simply because they have parents who put the highest priority on giving them the best upbringing and education in their power – and these are precisely the children who can make the best possible use of Oxbridge places. Instead they are barred by a kind of underhand and secretive ideological conspiracy, operating behind closed doors. It is characteristic of this current form of social engineering that, although it involves large sums of taxpayers' money, it operates without any statutory authority whatever.

This kind of positive discrimination or, to give it its true name, political bias, operates informally at many levels of our society today. It is ubiquitous in the Labour Party, where equality of opportunity is now threatened not only in the selection of parliamentary candidates but in the Leader of the Opposition's choice of front-bench colleagues. Some back-bench Labour MPs bitterly resent the way women get automatic promotion solely because of their sex and in 1993 took a furtive revenge by voting one of them off the Shadow Cabinet list. But none dared take an open stand on the grounds of equity and justice. Why? It is as though huge sections of our society have been brainwashed and coerced into Political Correctness, the new and debilitating scourge which has replaced Marxism.

Similar trends are to be seen even in the Conservative Party. When Douglas Hurd entered the contest for the Tory leadership in 1990, he and his team were at pains to belittle, explain away or hush up the fact that he had been to Eton. Why should he be ashamed of his old school, which has a splendid record of attainment in many fields? Again, when I suggested in 1993 that the Tory Party, which plainly needed a new chairman, should consider Nicholas Soames MP, because he had exactly the right mixture of jovial enthusiasm and the gift for making people feel good which the party's low spirits needed, I was told this was impossible. Oh yes, said high-placed Tories to me, we agree that Nicholas is just the man for the job. But – an Old Etonian, a former Guards officer, a friend of Prince Charles, the son of a peer, Churchill's grandson, a chap who's inherited money, etc., etc. – it just isn't on. Why, the fellow's a gentleman, he believes in honour, probity, *noblesse oblige*, all those forbidden things! Such arguments by no means affect only the top echelons of the party. It is now commonplace for a man or woman to be ruled out as constituency chairman simply because of associations with land, wealth or title.

This pursuit of greyness, this preference for the undistin-guished and indistinguishable, is spreading like a disease through our society. We live in a country which has grown great by our willingness to confer power on eccentric and difficult genius. Told that Wolfe was mad, George III replied: 'Then I wish he would bite some of my other generals.' Their inability to meet the Grey Standard would have ruled out for public service Raleigh and Oliver Cromwell, both Pitts, Palmerston, Gladstone and Disraeli, and of course Lloyd George and Churchill, the men who led us to victory in two world wars. It is no accident that the first Prime Minister chosen because he was dull, safe and grey, Stanley Baldwin, sleepwalked his way into the catastrophes of the 1930s. Equally, great, flamboyant or exceptional women like Queen Elizabeth I, Florence Nightingale or George Eliot would have been unable to meet our current requirements for pallid mediocrity. The fall of Margaret Thatcher in 1990 was an exercise in levelling by grey men driven by fear and envy of an outsize personality. Most of them, I note, had their origins in south Wales, an area notorious for resentment towards the successful, for grudge-bearing and back-stabbing.

For anyone familiar with British history, it is hard to believe that this new cult of mediocrity is deep-rooted, so alien is it to our traditions and national temperament. And certainly there is no evidence that ordinary people want greyness. We are nearing the end of the first century of the common man. But all experience suggests that the common man, given the choice, does not want to be ruled by common men but by uncommon men – and uncommon women too. Margaret Thatcher was thrice chosen Prime Minister by the people, and if she was not allowed to fight a fourth time it was not their choice. She was pushed aside in panic – and, as it turned out, quite needless panic – by her mediocre colleagues. The people were allowed no part in it. Thus one of the most exciting and fruitful periods in modern British history was brought to an end in a thoroughly undemocratic manner.

The people, then, do not want greyness. But they may have greyness thrust upon them. There are ominous signs that, unless we act to prevent it, our country may only be beginning to enter the Grey Age. For, in addition to the forces of greyness already powerful in Britain, we must now cope increasingly with the deadening weight of the Grey Continent. The European Community, whatever its idealistic origins, is now about greyness, congruity, sameness, homogeneity, conformity and levelling. The notion of competition has been turned on its head. Wherever possible, industry and agriculture all over Europe are being made to fit into a Procrustean Bed designed by bureaucrats. The only way to escape the attentions of Brussels is to conform exactly to specifications laid down in hundreds of thousands of regulations, often of mind-wrenching obscurity. In February 1994, for instance, Brussels imposed a fine of £27 million upon the British Steel Corporation, the most successful steel company in Europe, celebrated for its un-rivalled record in raising output per man-hour. Studying the impenetrable language in which the Brussels verdict is couched, I found that the only real complaint the Commission had against British Steel was that it was highly productive and efficient and so made large profits. It put to shame other EC steel producers, most of which require large subsidies to stay in business. So it was fined and told to level itself down to the rest.

The regulation of every aspect of production, even of life itself, by officials whose entire *raison d'être* is to devise uniform shapes, sizes, methods, flavours, textures and qualities, and then enforce them, has now become the object for which the Community exists. Christopher Booker's book gives scores of examples of Brussels' insanity in enforcing its diktats. Many of them are very funny and we laugh at them. But after we have laughed, the officials continue to enforce their rules, however risible, and British businessmen, farmers, fishermen and manufacturers are compelled to obey them, often at huge expense and to the detriment of their products. There is no case that I know of where Brussels has been defeated by laughter. Brussels does not possess a sense of humour – perhaps fortunately, because if it did it would impose it on the rest of us. We may smile at the efforts of the bureaucrats to produce a straight cucumber, but the dismal fact is that Brussels has already succeeded in eliminating scores of traditional British types of apple, which may no longer be marketed and so are now rarely grown. These prohibitions will eventually affect thousands of products, most of them developed precisely because they are found useful or palatable or cheap or convenient by ordinary people. The latest target for Brussels uniformity is the double-decker bus. London's scarlet double-deckers are famous all over the world and are one of the best features of our capital. They are economical, efficient and popular – and much envied on the Continent. They are not, as it happens, all that old, going back only to the double-deck horse-drawn omnibus of the late 1820s, which actually was first introduced in Paris (Pascal called for their introduction as far back as the seventeenth century). But only Britain and Ireland now have them, and Brussels insists this eccentricity must cease, on grounds of 'safety'.

Half a century ago, such assaults by foreign officials on much-loved British institutions would have seemed inconceivable. Indeed, it is difficult to imagine them occurring even twenty years ago. It is depressing how quickly and surely we are being gauleitered into submission. When I complain of such oppression to friends in Italy or Greece, they are amazed. 'If you don't like Brussels regulations, why do you obey them?' they ask. They are genuinely puzzled. They come from countries with no tradition of freedom where authority has always been oppressive and its orders therefore circumvented, disobeyed or resisted. The idea of a country like Britain, where the form of government is reached by popular consent, where Parliament is elected to pursue the *res publica* and its laws are therefore respected and obeyed, is quite alien to them. For them, power has always been a conspiracy against the people, who have learned over the centuries how to protect themselves. In France, where most of these unifying regulations have their origins, powerful interests have long been accustomed to defy authority by a *fronde*, an *émeute*, or, if necessary, by revolution. Despite its various constitutions, France has remained a bureaucratic oligarchy punctuated by popular reigns of terror, and ordinary Frenchmen view Brussels as they have always viewed Paris. In January 1994 French fishermen objected to fish imports into Brittany, made possible by new European Union regulations, by the simple expedient of burning down the warehouses which contained them. The French government did nothing. In France *le pouvoir* discriminates between violence which affects its vital interests and 'popular anger' which merely hurts someone else. The fish came from Britain and Spain, so its destruction was of no interest to the *préfecture*. Of course there are risks in this policy. The habit of using violence when you do not like the law is catching, especially in a country like France which has a long tradition of taking to the streets. Students, farmers, lorry-drivers, airport staff – more and more groups in French society have recently gained their ends by using force on a large scale, thus inciting others to do the same. This is likely to end in anarchy and the fall of the régime, as has happened so often in the past when weak French governments have surrendered to the mob. Meanwhile, France is on the list of EU members where Brussels is obeyed only when it suits the vested interests.

In Britain, with our different traditions, laws are routinely enforced and obeyed. Traditionally we have regarded the law as just, even when sometimes misguided, and those who enforce it not as enemies or even as bureaucrats but as civil servants doing their duty. But a change is coming, and a change infinitely for the worse, for all of us. The mindfix of Brussels is contagious. What we are beginning to see is the British civil service cooperating enthusiastically with the Brussels bureaucrats in the business of oppression. When Christopher Booker began his investigations into the steady increase in regulations strangling our economic life, he discovered 'a disturbing number of instances where much of the damage being caused by EU directives was coming not from the original directives themselves but from the way they were being implemented by the civil servants in Whitehall as they drew up the regulations putting them into UK law'. He found, further, that many of the worst cases of reglementary insanity sprang not so much from Brussels itself as from the spread of the infection here. In short, Continental authoritarianism is now inextricably mingled with the effects of the huge statutes pushed through

Parliament by the lobbies and pressure groups in the 1980s and since, which I have listed on page 102. All these laws are being enforced with relentless inflexibility, and with total disregard for their financial effects on individuals and the economy, by British civil servants who have interpreted our merging with Europe as the opening of a new era of power and expansion for their caste. It is a horrific prospect.

One danger is that the British will not indefinitely submit to bureaucratic destruction of their businesses, jobs and livelihoods. Seeing what the Continentals do, they will imitate them, by mass disobedience of the law, by the bribing of officials or, most likely, by organised violence. That will be tragic for us all. The rule of law is the most valuable of all our national assets, from which we benefit in countless different ways. Once undermined, we all suffer. Then again, Britain has not had the experience of settling things by violence for three and a half centuries. The last occasion, the civil war of the 1640s, was an avoidable disaster, a calamity without parallel in our history in its destruction of life, property and all that is most precious in an ordered and settled society. That mistake must never be repeated. At all costs, we must avoid becoming a country where violence or the threat of it is part of the regular vocabulary of politics.

I say 'at all costs': but of course there comes a point, in the history of any society, when the cost of submitting to wrong and destructive politics becomes, literally, unbearable. Then violence ensues inexorably, whatever the consequences. There is an increasing number of worrying features about Britain's whole European policy. Until recently, the follies of Brussels bureaucrats were seen as the acceptable price of attaching ourselves to what was regarded as European dynamism. The economic performance of the original six European Community states in their first quarter-century of cooperation was impressive. That of course was what persuaded Britain to turn its back on the Commonwealth, dissolve the European Free Trade Area, and go through the humiliation of soliciting entry to the EC in the face of de Gaulle's repeated vetos.

But since then there has been a sinister change in Europe's fortunes. Throughout the 1980s and still more so in the 1990s, growth rates have slowed. The dynamism has slowly been stilled. Compared with the economies of the Far East and South East Asia, and even with the United States, the twelve members of the EU have done poorly. Their record has been particularly unimpressive in job creation. Indeed it is doubtful if any new jobs have been created, in aggregate, over the past decade in the EU. With old jobs disappearing as industry absorbs labour-saving technology, the result is unemployment, which has been growing steadily for two decades and is now above the 10-per-cent level in EU states. In some of them it is much higher – in Spain nearly 18 per cent, for example. France, which traditionally had very low unemployment, now has about 12 per cent. In eastern Germany the level is about 20 per cent.

This growing lack of dynamism has been aggravated by EU policies, particularly the stress on regulations, labour welfare and work conditions. All these were adding steadily to European costs even before the Social Chapter was introduced. This, when fully implemented, is expected to add at least another 10 per cent to industrial costs generally. Particularly hard hit has been Germany, once the main engine of dynamism within the EU, where wage costs and social costs are now among the highest in the world, with increasingly serious consequences for German competitiveness in overseas markets. German industry, despite high investment, has found it more and more difficult to absorb increased costs. In the twelve-year period 1979–91, for instance, German productivity (output per capita) rose only 18 per cent (admittedly from a high base), against 30 per cent during the same period in France, Belgium and Denmark.

Significantly, during these years, British productivity rose by a massive 53 per cent. This was due to a combination of trade union reforms, privatisation, deregulation, holding down wage-costs and reducing unnecessary financial burdens on industry. In January 1994, the German Economics Minister, Gunther Rexrodt, presenting his annual report on the economy, drew attention to the results produced by the application of Thatcherite industrial policies in Britain. The achievements in reducing burdens on industry, he said, were 'outstanding' in Britain, which had produced 'exceptional results in breaking down bureaucratic obstacles to starting up new businesses and managing existing companies'. A case in point has been the comparative performance of British car manufacturers, which in the thirty years 1950–80 had fallen well behind their German competitors, or had simply disappeared. But in 1993 Rover sold 387,000 cars in Europe, compared to 345,000 for Mercedes and 321,000 for BMW (both figures up to November 1993). As a result BMW was driven to the drastic step of buying Rover for £800 million in February 1994. This is part of a pattern in which successful manufacturing nations like Japan, Germany and the United States are building plants in Britain to take advantage of low wage costs, rising productivity and relatively light regulation. But of course this temporary advantage will be thrown away if we allow our competitive position to be eroded by bureaucratic soporifics, both home-grown and imported from Brussels, and if we are forced to implement the Social Chapter, like the other eleven EU states.

The question therefore arises: in becoming a member of the EU has Britain, once again, joined the wrong show? It certainly begins to seem like it. The focus and fulcrum of the world economy is shifting away from Europe and the North Atlantic to East Asia and the Pacific. Europe, unless it changes its bureaucratic and socialist ways, is in danger of becoming an economic backwater by the end of this decade, carrying Britain with it. And we ourselves will find all the Thatcherite reforms useless if regulation, subsidies and state interference return via Brussels. A case in point is the airline business. Most of the best airlines are now concentrated in the Far East. But the United States remains extremely competitive chiefly because of its size and the opportunities for new businesses to start up. In 1993 alone, for instance, four major new airlines opened up for service there. In this world league, the only competitive EU airline is British Airways. This is due entirely to the structural reforms carried out in the airline before and since privatisation, which included shedding half its workforce while actually increasing the number of miles flown and passengers carried. This, then, was a typical Thatcherite success story of de-regulation and freedom from state interference. In 1992, British

Airways was one of the few major airlines in the world to make a
profit – nearly $300 million. By contrast, eight out of nine EC
state airlines (Alitalia, Air France, Aer Lingus, Lufthansa,
TAP [Portugal], KLM, Iberia and Olympic [Greece]) all
made losses, which in aggregate amounted to $2172 million
(Sabena made a theoretical profit of $12 million). The profit-
and-loss figures for 1993 will show a still greater difference in
performances between British Airways and the rest. And all
this has happened despite the huge state subsidies paid to the
Continental airlines – $5 billion in 1991/2, and about $6 billion
in the current year. All these subsidies require, and get, EC
approval.

Obviously, if the EU really pursued the competition policies
to which it is theoretically committed, most, perhaps all, of
these national flag carriers would be driven out of business.
Indeed, with the exception of Lufthansa and Sabena, it is
doubtful if any of them could survive once privatised. That is
precisely the solution recommended by an EU report published
in February 1994, which cited British Airways as the model
other EU lines should follow. But exactly the same argument
could and should have been used in the case of the EU steel
industries. Instead, British Steel, the efficient market leader,
was condemned and fined. The fear is that Brussels will apply
the same kind of perverted logic to airlines and haul BA into the
dock for punishment. That, at the moment, is how the
European Union works.

The problem for Britain is to decide whether it has tied itself
to a moribund entity which will drift slowly downwards into
industrial dependency, and so require high external tariffs to
survive at all – an entity for which there can be no long-term
future – or whether, given strong leadership, it is still possible to
reinvigorate the European Union. The prospects for the second
may not be quite as gloomy as they seem at present, for Europe
itself is entering a period of political flux. The old Christian
Democrat/Social Democrat condominium is breaking down
everywhere, voters are turning against the consensus politics
of the past half-century which made the EU possible, new
parties are springing up and nothing can now be ruled out. This
holds grave dangers, of course. The extreme right is gaining

ground everywhere, both outside traditional parties and within them, fed by the rising hatred of immigrants from the east and south. In Italy the country, heartily sickened by its corrupt political elites, is polarising into far left and far right, with a strong possibility that a Mussolini-like solution will be adopted. Germany, where the attempt to integrate the East without trouble or tears has manifestly failed, could go the same way, as the Christian Democrat régime draws to its close. In France, where the government is weak, the forces of anarchy strong and the habit of making concessions to mob violence well established, the preconditions for revolution are present. Spain is another fragile case, with exceptionally high unemployment and ubiquitous corruption, where the strongest institution now, oddly enough, is the monarchy. It is the view of the Brussels political strategists – in so far as such people exist – that the outlook for Europe's federalist centre is so gloomy that the only viable policy is to rush headlong towards union, with a single currency on the immediate agenda. That seems to me a formula for catastrophe, especially since a European currency is unacceptable to the German people and likely to tip the scales there in favour of right-wing nationalism.

However, the European flux also offers opportunities for Britain. What Europeans seem to want, in overwhelming numbers, is not federalism or right-wing nationalism or anything desperate or drastic. What they want is democracy: governments which listen to them, respond to them and attempt to satisfy their reasonable demands. Britain is in many ways well suited to lead Europe back to democracy. It is our ancient habit to assemble and direct European coalitions against threats to the independence and liberties of its people – against the Habsburgs in the sixteenth century, against the Bourbons in the seventeenth century, against revolutionary and Bonapartist France in the eighteenth and nineteenth centuries, against the Hohenzollerns and the Nazis in the twentieth century, and finally against the Soviets. We are accustomed to starting in a minority of one and ending at the head of a grand array of nations. It is indeed exactly fifty years ago that Britain was the home port of the vast international armada which sailed to Normandy to liberate Europe – having,

only four years before, stood absolutely alone. There would be
nothing new in Britain beginning a crusade to make the
European Union democratic.

But to do that, Britain must first make its own democracy
work. At the moment it is plainly failing the nation. We live not
in a working democracy but in a pseudo-democracy, where the
forms are carried out and the content is lacking. Never in my
lifetime has discontent with our political system been so
widespread and despairing – with a hint of rising anger too. All
our major institutions are going through hard times but
Parliament is perhaps in the most serious trouble. The Prime
Minister has no authority. Most people hold him in contempt.
They regard the Leader of the Opposition as a nonentity,
usually invisible. Three-quarters of the people believe ministers
habitually lie. Two-thirds categorise the Conservatives as 'the
party of sleaze'. A similar proportion have no confidence in
Labour's ability to govern. It is hard to recall a period in which
MPs have aroused less esteem. There was a time, not so long
ago, where ordinary constituents, irrespective of party, were
proud to shake their MP by the hand and have a few words of
conversation – would talk about it for weeks and remember it
for years. Now it is regarded as a dubious distinction. The year
1993 was a vintage one for parliamentary scandals; 1994 began
with still more sleaze. These are mostly miserable affairs,
showing MPs as weak, silly, sadly limited and, at worst, squalid
and irresponsible, rather than corrupt or wicked. But their
cumulative effect – their drip-drip-drip eroding the public's
confidence and trust in their representatives – is deadly. The
public now places politicians only slightly above journalists in
their litany of loathing. That is new in Britain and deeply
disturbing.

Behind this collapse in confidence is of course the evidence of
the democratic failure which is the theme of this book.
Obviously, if the people now believe they get their way on
virtually nothing, they hold Parliament in general, and
individual MPs in particular, responsible. Who else are they to
blame? But there is a widespread feeling that the party system is
also at fault. 'All the parties are the same' – never before has this
remark been so common. And like most common observations,

it is founded in truth. The whole virtue of the party system, which has many disagreeable and disgusting features, is that it enables the voters to exercise clear choices over a wide range of issues. If it fails to do that, better to scrap it. And it is failing. Labour has virtually ceased to be a socialist party and has deliberately drawn nearer the Conservatives on defence, foreign policy and the economy. It is now even trying to set itself up as the party of low taxation. Major and Smith disagree on very little and their indignant sparring across the Dispatch Box looks increasingly contrived. Their main point of difference lies in who ought to sit on the Treasury bench. In fact, forty years on, Butskellism (coined from an amalgam of R. A. Butler and Hugh Gaitskell, in charge of Tory and Labour economic policy respectively) has made its reappearance in the shape of a new political amalgam, or rather two. There is Smith Major, a sort of gangling teenager from a pre-war minor public school. Or Major Smith, a pernickety old dugout in the Royal Army Ordinance Corps. Neither is the stuff of greatness, or even outstanding mediocrity. Then, to complete this political Tom, Dick and Harry, there is Paddy Ashdown, who brings to mind a famous phrase of the great Lord Curzon's, 'a person of the utmost insignificance'. Major, Smith, Ashdown – the century of the common man is certainly ending true to form.

The point on which the three party leaderships not merely agree, but coagulate, is Europe. All are enthusiastic supporters of British membership. All helped to push Maastricht through Parliament. All welcome the transformation of the Community into the Union. All believe in federalism, though they may not actually use the term. Whether the rank and file of the three parties, let alone those who vote for them, share the European ardour of their leadership is another matter. The polls suggest otherwise. But the fact is that all three parties are now committed to the European course, so the electors have no choice at all.

We have here strong, democratic grounds for breaking up the existing party system, as is happening elsewhere in Europe. Each of the three parties, in any case, is already operating under false pretences. Labour has fulfilled the historic purposes for which it was created in 1900 and wants to cut itself off from its trade union roots – is doing so, indeed, as fast as it can find alternative finance. 'Conservative' is a misnomer for a party led by men who want to dissolve British sovereignty in a European superstate and thus carry through the most radical change in a millennium. The Liberal Democrats bear no relation whatever to the historic party of Gladstone or even of Asquith. The most striking feature of all three groups is now their federalism, and it is as components of a new Federal Party that they ought to come together.

That would open the way for a new party to emerge. It would be broadly conservative in its attitudes, campaign for the retention of essential elements of British sovereignty, and so offer opponents of federalism an alternative to vote for. Equally important, it could assume the leadership in Europe of the countless millions of people who likewise reject federalism and who stand for what President de Gaulle called *l'Europe des patries*. Such a new party is not only essential to reinvigorate democracy in Britain – and then in Europe; it is also urgently needed to forestall a resurgence of the authoritarian right, which could break out here as well as on the Continent. Nationalism can be civilised, democratic and constructive. Or it can be brutal, despotic and destructive. We can ensure that it is the former only by giving the forces of nationalism, which exist and are growing, a genuine outlet within the democratic spectrum. That should be the first task. I call on elements within the Conservative Party, and men and women of good will and foresight outside it, to put their heads together and see how quickly such a new party can be brought into being.

At the same time, we must be thinking much further ahead. We will soon be entering a new century, which promises to be even more exciting and shocking than the old one, as the speed of technological change accelerates. Among other things, it is likely to force upon us fundamental readjustments in the way we engage in politics. The question is, whether we plan these readjustments sensibly or just allow them to happen. It is absurd to think that, when everything else changes, the way we play the political game will remain the same. In the days of the Greek city-state, the entire free male population could participate directly in political decision-making, assembled in the same spot, just as they could all attend the games together. In medieval England, the first true nation-state, towns and shires selected representatives and sent them to Westminster, a nation of two or three million delegating its authority to a few hundred. That, broadly speaking, is the system that has been followed ever since, by every country in the world which practises democracy.

We have seen, however, that it is breaking down in Britain as the pressure groups and the lobbies and the single-issue fanatics take over from the people. Similar complaints are heard virtually everywhere. Moreover, the representational form of democracy, the one forced upon us by the tyranny of distance, is no longer the sole alternative. I think we will need representational politics for the foreseeable future to perform many functions, including the actual business of government. But many aspects of policy-making and even legislation will soon be transacted, if we so choose, by direct consultation with the entire adult population. There is nothing entirely new in this. You could say it is a return to the Greek city-state system of direct democracy but on a colossal scale. You could also argue it is an adaptation of the Swiss method which has been in use for over a century. Swiss citizens directly determine many matters, of acute interest to every voter, which in other countries are delegated to parliaments. They vote, for instance, on whether a visitor can become a Swiss citizen – a power hundreds of millions of Europeans would dearly love to possess. In February 1994 the Swiss electorate, overruling its federal parliament and the all-powerful European transport lobbies, made it obligatory for foreign lorries crossing Switzerland to travel by train. This is mighty awkward for the authorities in Berne and may be in breach of all kinds of international conventions. But it is democracy in action.

The Swiss system, so suitable for a little country of four nationalities placed awkwardly across the Alps – and so successful too, since Switzerland is among the most contented countries in the world and its people are certainly among the richest – will soon be open to all. When I was a member of the British Cable Authority in the 1980s, helping to lay down the rules under which the country is being 'cabled up', it seemed to

me, as I learned the immense, almost limitless, possibilities of
fibre-optic cables, that a new chapter in political democracy
was opening. These cables are not merely receptive but inter-
active. They link us all together and each of us to the centre, or
many centres. The Americans call them 'information super-
highways'. But they are much more than that. They are not just
a new invention but, like printing, they open up a distinct epoch
in world history. Over years and decades and generations they
will change our lives in all kinds of fundamental ways, some not
yet foreseen. And they will certainly change our political
system. As countries are cabled up, it will be possible to hold,
once a week, say at 7 pm on a Friday evening, a meeting of the
entire nation, in which we can consult together and decide what
to do. We can also hold meetings, so flexible is the system, of an
entire county, town, district or parish. Indeed, it is peculiarly
well suited to meeting the needs of regional and local government. I have said little of local democracy in this book, but it is
undoubtedly true that most of the arguments used to criticise
the workings of the national system apply even more forcibly at
the local level, where popular anger at the breakdown of the
democratic process in the town halls is beginning to overflow.
This is due, in part, to the laziness and indifference of voters
who will not turn out at local elections (often because they have
no hope of overthrowing a built-in Labour or Tory majority).
But people who will not cast general votes in elections will
easily be persuaded to participate in direct consultation over
specific and burning local issues, especially if they can do so
from the comfort of their own homes.

Thus one of the greatest frustrations of modern democracy
will be removed. Just as market democracy enables all of us to
vote with our purses every day of our lives, so electronic
democracy will make it possible for us to vote with our ballots
not just once in five years but as often as we decide is desirable.
Parliaments and local government bodies will naturally
remain, and function in many ways as they do at present. But
electronic democracy will supplement the elective system,
adding a new dimension of universal participation in the
settlement of key issues. In the coming age, we will have a grand
debate on how exactly and how often this new process will be

used. We may well have to proceed at first by trial and error. Electronic democracy need not be a case of the ignorant multitude taking decisions in place of the informed assembly. The whole essence of the system is that it conveys information as well as registers decisions. We can be told, as each issue comes up, the nature and consequences of the range of choices open to us, and given information about them in whatever quantity each of us desires. Then we can make up our minds, and there will be no fudging the results because they will flash up instantaneously on our screens.

Many people will recoil from this prospect in horror, just as Sir Robert Peel and the Duke of Wellington and thousands of other sensible and good men recoiled in horror from the Great Reform Bill of 1832. There are plenty of people in Britain today, in all three parties and in every class, including the chattering ones, who pay lip-service to democracy but dislike intensely any attempt to make it function properly. They don't want their elitist attitudes and prejudices overruled by the common people. The truth is, in their hearts they distrust and even hate the people. I have no such fears and inhibitions. I believe the hearts of the British are sound, their judgements are usually right, their brains are as sharp and their muscles as strong as ever. They deserve democracy – and they ought to get it. In a few years' time they *will* get it, in all its plentitude.

In the meantime, there is much to do. Britain is a dispirited and pessimistic society today and with reason. Decisions which ought to be ours are taken out of our hands completely by bureaucrats in Brussels or in Whitehall. Parliament is controlled not by the voters but by lobbies and pressure groups. The legislation it enacts reflects their views, not ours. We are being slowly but inexorably sucked into a federalist vortex which few of us want and most of us emphatically reject. We live, as it were, in an occupied country in which more and more decisions are taken by tiny, unrepresentative, unelected groups, mostly hidden and some almost totally unknown, secretive, arrogant and usually misguided oligarchies, people we cannot confront.

There are things we can do quickly. A new party structure I have already indicated. That will revitalise the House of

Commons and make it more responsive. The House of Lords, that ridiculous body, should be replaced by an entirely elected body, though a much smaller one, specifically vested with wide powers to correct the abuses of the lobby system and ensure that legislation reflects the popular will. This new Upper House will also, as does the Senate in the United States, reflect the interests of the regions, now often ignored or overruled or represented entirely by narrow and self-centred pressure groups. Here will be our democratic long-stop, always there when the Commons fails in its duty. Thus we will prepare ourselves for the direct democracy that is coming.

However, none of this will make the essential difference if the British people remain comatose. Parliamentary democracy, market democracy, electronic democracy all demand an active, wide-awake *demos*. The people must be up and about. Are they? Not at the moment. There is a general feeling of lassitude and defeatism in Britain today. Too many people shrug their shoulders and predict 'they' can't be beaten. 'They' have the money. 'They' control the media. 'They' run big business or the parties or the ministries or the town halls. So what's the use, mate? Better let 'them' get on with it, while the rest of us look after number one. That, of course, is just the attitude 'they' want to encourage. 'They' like a sheepish people, tamely trotting in and out of the pens determined by the lobbies and pressure groups, the men from the ministry, the men from Brussels, the corrupt or suborned MPs, the tame media hacks, the experts and the knowalls, the secretive men and women on committees who know what's good for the rest of us, the ministers who have been too long in power and who think the people are trash, the PROs and image-makers and advertising specialists – those clever, well-placed and smug oligarchs who think we are all putty in their capable, none-too-clean hands. They want us to believe they will always be on top, that the rule of 'them' is for ever.

That is nonsense. It is a myth that 'they' cannot be pushed aside by the people. I have lived most of my adult life among the elites and the rulers and the opinion-formers and, with remarkably few exceptions, I have found them mediocre. They survive and set the tone and give the orders simply because we allow them to do so, because the people, as G. K. Chesterton put it, 'never have spoken yet'. For the most part, these self-appointed, self-perpetuating elites are neither clever nor wise, nor daring, nor vigorous, nor courageous. Above all, not courageous. They are lath-and-plaster men, cardboard cut-outs, aping a genuine ruling class. They award each other absurd gongs and false distinctions, honorary degrees which are often themselves marks of dishonour; they pay each other salaries from the public purse, appoint each other to sinecures and cosy perches, exchange resonant titles – 'My Right Honourable Friend', 'Your Lordships', 'The learned and gallant member', 'Minister', 'Vice-Chancellor', 'Chairman', 'Secretary of State', 'Mr President' – and greedily divide the spoils and the jobs. But there is not much fight in them. Most of them are conformists at heart, secure in a body, lost when alone, quick to take alarm, constantly looking over their shoulders, easily panicked. Cold steel, hot blood, a whiff of grapeshot, the roar of the mob – it is amazing how many things scare them. It will not take much – or many – to get them on the run.

So the people should be of good heart. To get the democracy which is their right, they do not need to overcome a determined, ruthless body of hard men who will fight to the last ditch and die where they stand. There are no such creatures in charge of Britain now: the acropolis is in the hands of a garrison grown fat and lazy with easy pickings and soft options, not well led but badly disciplined, lacking a cause to fight for. One fierce assault from the *demos* and the white flag will flutter.

But we must attack soon, while the citadel is still worth taking, while Britain still has an economy that can be saved and a sovereignty fit to fight for and a way of life to be rescued. To the old I say: don't leave us without one last effort to save the country you have loved and served. To the middle-aged the message is: give us leadership, brains, wise counsel and your substance – without you, nothing can be done. To the young, I exhort: the country you will live in for the rest of your lives is what you make it now, by your energy and spirit and ardour. We are all in this together, but it is youth, with longest to enjoy or endure, who have most to lose by inaction and slumber.

Thus I find, as I move into old age, my concern for my own prospects is vanishing but my anxieties about what will face my children, and still more my grandchildren, have sharply increased. It would be ignoble as well as complacent to say, 'It will last my time.' The real question is: 'Will it last their time?' And the answer, at present, is no. We have to see our country not just as a habitation but as an inheritance, something handed on to us for our lifetimes, to be protected, cherished, preserved, if possible enriched and improved – then, when our turn comes, handed on intact to our successors. I often think of my Victorian and Edwardian forebears and what they and their generation left mine: my maternal grandfather, for instance, an enthusiastic supporter of Mr Gladstone and treasurer of his memory; my great-uncle James, who sorrowfully voted against Mr Balfour in the 1906 election – over free trade – and helped to lose that unfortunate gentleman his seat. What a strong, secure and honourable country they bequeathed to us – and how diminished, fragile and tawdry it seems today!

There are some odd continuities. One of the pleasures I share with my four grandchildren is to sit in my library and watch videos from my Laurel and Hardy collection. My grandchildren's delight in the innocent clowning of these two gifted buffoons is just as keen as mine was, when I first watched these same films in the mid-1930s. We sit there in a row laughing together, and anticipating the next catastrophe, for we know some of these comedies by heart. But I can't help contrasting our predicaments. When I saw the originals of *Way Out West* and *Another Fine Mess* in 1935 or so, the world was not free from perils: sinister monster-clowns, in the shape of Hitler, Mussolini and Stalin, were setting the scene for real-life catastrophes in Europe. But Britain itself, the country of my childhood, remained robust, salubrious and sterling. We were proud of it. Then, to say that 'To be born English is to draw first prize in the lottery of life' was still true.

It is a different story today, and I tremble for those four small persons sitting by my side. The empire is gone, great-power status is gone, our sovereign parliament is going fast. We are merging our nation's identity with something quite unknown but which looks increasingly alien. And at home, all the innocence I knew has been invaded. My grandchildren will never be allowed to play freely in the street, as I did. They must be cautioned against all kinds of dangers which, in my childhood, simply did not exist. They will grow up wise, or at any rate knowing, before their time. The television set emits its endless litany of crime, sex, violence and gutter-speech. The newspapers tell, in specific detail, of the *EastEnders* star who gave 'blow-jobs' or the latest Member of Parliament to disgrace himself by 'auto-erotic asphyxiation'. Schools give them official guidance on 'sexual orientation'. The law tells them how they can 'divorce' their parents. They are growing up into a world which is unrestrained, foul-mouthed, garish, defiled, vicious and often plain evil.

But it need not happen. This is not the world the ordinary people of Britain want. Nor is it one they need endure. They still have the power, by a supreme reassertion of their democratic authority, to change it all and to bring Britain back to its old notions of honour, decency, prudence and self-restraint – and to restore its old skill in looking after its fundamental interests. But my grandchildren, growing up fast, remind me how urgent the need for transformation is.

So clang the alarm-bells! Wake up Britain!

Index